CAMBRIDGE LIBRARY COLLECTION

Books of enduring scholarly value

History

The books reissued in this series include accounts of historical events and movements by eye-witnesses and contemporaries, as well as landmark studies that assembled significant source materials or developed new historiographical methods. The series includes work in social, political and military history on a wide range of periods and regions, giving modern scholars ready access to influential publications of the past.

The Home of the Monk

First published twice in 1926, and again in 1934 with an updated bibliography, Cranage's *The Home of the Monk* is a small but useful introduction for the visitor to any English monastic site. Working from surviving architectural and documentary evidence, he examines the buildings section by section, explaining how each part of an abbey was used. He briefly explains the history of the various monastic orders which existed in medieval England, and their differences from one another. He also provides plans of what constituted the typical arrangements likely to be found in Benedictine, Augustinian, Cluniac and Cistercian houses. The book provides a useful starting point for further study of medieval religious houses, and a handy guide for the occasional visitor to such sites.

Cambridge University Press has long been a pioneer in the reissuing of out-of-print titles from its own backlist, producing digital reprints of books that are still sought after by scholars and students but could not be reprinted economically using traditional technology. The Cambridge Library Collection extends this activity to a wider range of books which are still of importance to researchers and professionals, either for the source material they contain, or as landmarks in the history of their academic discipline.

Drawing from the world-renowned collections in the Cambridge University Library, and guided by the advice of experts in each subject area, Cambridge University Press is using state-of-the-art scanning machines in its own Printing House to capture the content of each book selected for inclusion. The files are processed to give a consistently clear, crisp image, and the books finished to the high quality standard for which the Press is recognised around the world. The latest print-on-demand technology ensures that the books will remain available indefinitely, and that orders for single or multiple copies can quickly be supplied.

The Cambridge Library Collection will bring back to life books of enduring scholarly value (including out-of-copyright works originally issued by other publishers) across a wide range of disciplines in the humanities and social sciences and in science and technology.

The Home
of the Monk

*An Account of English Monastic Life
and Buildings in the Middle Ages*

David Herbert Somerset Cranage

CAMBRIDGE
UNIVERSITY PRESS

CAMBRIDGE UNIVERSITY PRESS

Cambridge, New York, Melbourne, Madrid, Cape Town, Singapore,
São Paolo, Delhi, Dubai, Tokyo

Published in the United States of America by Cambridge University Press, New York

www.cambridge.org
Information on this title: www.cambridge.org/9781108013376

© in this compilation Cambridge University Press 2010

This edition first published 1934
This digitally printed version 2010

ISBN 978-1-108-01337-6 Paperback

The Home of the Monk

LONDON
Cambridge University Press
FETTER LANE

NEW YORK · TORONTO
BOMBAY · CALCUTTA · MADRAS
Macmillan

TOKYO
Maruzen Company Ltd

PLATE I

CHESTER. FRATER PULPIT

The Home of the Monk

AN ACCOUNT
OF ENGLISH MONASTIC LIFE
AND BUILDINGS IN THE
MIDDLE AGES

by

THE VERY REV.
D. H. S. CRANAGE
Litt.D., F.S.A., Hon.A.R.I.B.A.
Dean of Norwich

Cambridge
AT THE UNIVERSITY PRESS
MCMXXXIV

First Edition . . . . . *July*   1926
Second Edition . . . . . *December* 1926
Third Edition . . . . . *March*   1934

PRINTED IN GREAT BRITAIN

TO
MY WIFE

Preface

THE object of this little book is to attract the ordinary reader to the subject of English monastic buildings. I have begun, therefore, with the cloister as the centre of daily life, and have put off till towards the end a general sketch of monastic history and an account of the various Orders. The title of the book is not strictly accurate, as the regular canons as well as the monks are included. The life and buildings of the two bodies, however, have so many points in common that it is impossible to treat them separately. The friars are scarcely mentioned, for their origin and ideals, and to some extent their buildings, are very different from those of the monks.

Monastic life is so closely connected with monastic buildings, and adds so much human interest to them, that I have borne it constantly in mind. It may be objected that there are too many quotations, but all are from original authorities. The student of mediaeval monasteries must, for all time, be indebted mainly to the Rule of St Benedict, *The Rites of Durham*, and the Customaries of various houses. It has seemed to me far more interesting to give the actual words of these, or translations, rather than to attempt paraphrases of them. I have made very full use of Mr J. W. Clark's delightful book on Barnwell, through the kindness of

Preface

his son, Mr E. Mellish Clark, and his publisher's son, Mr G. Brimley Bowes. Acknowledgments of other help received will be found in the descriptions of the plans and photographs.

The plans are chosen to illustrate, in as normal a manner as possible, the conventual arrangements of the Benedictine, Cluniac, and Cistercian Orders, and of the regular canons. Many details are, of necessity, omitted, and no attempt is made, in using such a small scale, to shew the dates of the various parts. The descriptions give these dates in broad outline. The photographs are of course not so numerous as I should have liked, but again the size of the book has to be borne in mind: most of them have not been published before.

The bibliography is obviously not exhaustive, but is designed, like the rest of the book, to help the general reader. I have kept the pages entirely free from footnotes, but the bibliography will nearly always indicate the source of the quotations.

D. H. S. C.

May, 1926

Note on the Second Edition

I am grateful for the various suggestions by re-viewers: slight corrections have been made accordingly. Mr G. G. Coulton believes that the famous plan found at St Gall was a fancy drawing of an ideal monastery, which was never carried out at St Gall or elsewhere. This seems to me very possible, but there is good evidence that the actual plan dates from the early part of the ninth century.

Mr Coulton is no doubt right in saying that *The Rites of Durham* should not be quoted without a caution, for it is an *ex parte* statement written perhaps half a century after the monastery was dissolved. Surely, however, it will always be a primary authority for the disposition and use of the buildings, and it is for this purpose almost entirely that I have quoted it.

D. H. S. C.

November, 1926

Note on the Third Edition

A few slight changes have been made and the Bibliography has been brought up to date.

D. H. S. C.

February, 1934

ix

Contents

Illustrations

Illustrations

Illustrations

PLATE II

NORWICH CATHEDRAL AND CLOISTER

The Home of the Monk

CHAPTER I

The Cloister

IN a very special sense the cloister was the home of
the monk. It was the secluded centre of his daily
life, communicating directly with the church and the
other chief buildings, and forming, in at least one of
its walks, the place of literary study.

The cloister was placed on the south side of the nave
of the church to secure the maximum of sunshine.
Occasionally the proximity of a road, or some other
local cause, made it desirable, for reasons of privacy,
that the cloister should be on the north side: notable
examples are Canterbury (Christ Church) and Chester.
At Waltham the unusual position was chosen of the
north side of the quire. There were four covered walks,
usually of about the same length and at right angles to
one another. Up to the thirteenth century at least the
roofs were supported on open arches, as may be seen
in the Norman drawing of Canterbury, now in the
Library of Trinity College, Cambridge: there are no
extensive remains of an English cloister of this period.
In the later Middle Ages glazed windows became the
rule instead of open arches. The cloister garth in the
centre was covered with grass.

All the walks were passages, but they had other uses
as well. At Durham the east and south "alleys" were

used for the ceremonies of Maundy Thursday. In the
east walk thirteen poor aged men sat on a broad thick
form, and, as we find from *The Rites of Durham*,

the Prior dyd washe the poore mens feete, all of theme, one after
an other, with his owne hands, and dryed them with a towell, and
kissed ther feite himeselfe, which being done he did verie liberally
bestowe xxx^d in money of every one of theme, with vij reade
herrings a pece, and did serve them him selfe with drinke and
iij loves of bread with certaine wafers.

In the south "alley" there was a long stone bench on
which a number of boys sat in a row and the

Monks dyd wash the said childryns feete, and dryed them with
a towell. Which being done, they dyd kisse the said childrins
fete, every one of those he washed, giving to every childe xxx^d
in money, and vij redde herrings and iij loves of bread and every
one certaine wafercakes, the Moncks serving every childe with
drinke themselves. The godly ceremony thus endyd, after
certaine praiers said by the Prior and the whole Covent, they dyd
all depart in great holynesse.

The south-east corner adjoining the entrance from
the courtyard beyond was the normal place for the
porter's seat. At each corner, and especially at the
north-east, there might be a bracket for a lamp. Such
a bracket remains at Lilleshall and elsewhere.

One of the walks, generally the west, was the novices'
schoolroom, and often retains evidence of its purpose
in the game boards scratched on the floor or benches.
Fox and goose and nine men's morris were evidently
played at Gloucester, and there are similar boards cut
in the stone at Westminster, Norwich, and Canterbury.
At Chester there are actually such marks inside the

church. The Master of the Novices was often an elderly man, and there may well have been occasions when a quiet game could be enjoyed without his knowing much about it. At Durham

one of the oldest Monnckes, that was lernede, was appointed to be there tuter....they never receyved wages, nor handled any money, in that space, but goynge daly to there bookes within the cloyster.

Boy novices are of course here referred to. If men applied for admission to a monastery, the greatest care had to be taken to test their vocation. The 58th chapter of the Rule of St Benedict describes the repeated delays and indignities which had to be endured by a newcomer before he could be received. At Barnwell enquiry was made as to his country, parentage, health, knowledge, behaviour, voice and power of singing, capacity for writing or of executing any mechanical art; whether he was in debt or had contracted other obligations; whether he was good-tempered, sociable, trustworthy and of good character; whether, in short, he was likely to be of use in the monastery.

The walk next the church, generally the north walk, was the most important, for it was the *scriptorium* of the monks. We know this to have been the case at many abbeys in the latter part of the Middle Ages. Presumably therefore it was the traditional position, though it is difficult to suppose that much reading and writing can have been done in Norman cloisters with arches open to the garth. The arrangement can be best understood by an examination of the beautiful cloister at Gloucester, erected at the end of the fourteenth century. Each four-light window had below it two little recesses projecting into the garth with separate single-light windows. At Durham there were

in every wyndowe iij PEWES or CARRELLS, where every one of the old Monks had his carrell, severall by himselfe, that, when they had dyned, they dyd resorte to that place of Cloister and there studied upon there books, every one in his carrell, all the after nonne, unto evensong tyme. This was there exercise every daie. All there pewes or carrells was all fynely wainscotted and verie close, all but the forepart which had carved wourke that gave light in at ther carrell doures of wainscott. And in every carrell was a deske to lye there bookes on.

On the floor was straw, hay, or mats for warmth and quietness, and at each end was a screen to keep off the draught and for privacy.

At Chester the walk next the church was wider than the others. It was not long enough to accommodate all the monks, and the carrells were therefore continued along part of the west walk.

There is very little evidence of the *scriptorium* being anywhere else but in the cloister, though we know that a special one was built at St Albans in the latter part of the fourteenth century. More than a hundred years before this, a large room was formed over the south aisle of the church at the Cluniac priory of Wenlock: it may well have been used as a *scriptorium*. The present cloister of Norwich was begun about 1300 and not finished till about 1450: its windows were not glazed. It seems very unlikely that the monks would be content to

4

PLATE III

GLOUCESTER. CLOISTER WALK NEXT THE CHURCH

use the north walk for their reading and writing, and I feel pretty confident that part of the upper storey, an unusual feature in an English abbey, was used as a *scriptorium*. At Evesham, too, we know that studies for monks over the east walk were formed between 1286 and 1316.

The few books owned by a monastery in the twelfth century were contained in cases against the wall near the north-east corner. In the Cistercian Order there was a book recess in the east wall, but soon a little room was formed near, also in the east walk. At Wenlock there is a large vaulted chamber of three bays in this position, dating from the beginning of the thirteenth century. At Worcester the room over the south aisle of the church was a library in the fourteenth century, and a special chamber was often built a hundred years later. At Bury and Norwich the library was probably over the cloister.

The number of books naturally increased as time went on. At Glastonbury there were 400 volumes in 1247. Bury had over 2000 before the Dissolution. Christ Church, Canterbury, was particularly rich. Before 1170 there were more than 600 volumes, about 1300 at least 1850, and at the Dissolution nearly 4000. To get at the actual number of works, one must multiply by about four, as several treatises were often contained in one volume. John Boston, a monk of Bury in 1410, compiled a catalogue of monastic libraries, visiting 195. At first the books were used only by monks of the house, but in the later Middle Ages all students were welcomed, and books were lent out on conditions.

The librarian, or *armarius*, was often the precentor. At Abingdon it was laid down that

when he is away, the succentor, if he be fit for the office, shall keep the library keys; but should he be giddy and light minded he shall give them to the prior or subprior.

Increasing care was taken of the library. At Barnwell, for instance, we are told that

the press in which the books are kept ought to be lined inside with wood, that the damp of the walls may not moisten or stain the books. This press should be divided vertically as well as horizontally by sundry shelves on which the books may be ranged so as to be separated from one another; for fear they be packed so close as to injure each other or delay those who want them.

Bury books still shew chain marks, and no doubt chaining was common, the books being read standing or sitting at desks near the shelves. Some books were kept in the church and the dining hall, as well as in the cloister and the library.

In speaking of monastic *scriptoria* and libraries, one naturally asks how far the monks were a learned body of men, but it is much too large a question to deal with fully here. It cannot, however, be passed over entirely. The Rule of St Benedict, in the 48th chapter, says that

at fixed times, the brothers ought to be occupied in manual labour; and, again, at fixed times, in sacred reading....Moreover on Sunday all shall engage in reading: excepting those who are deputed to various duties.

6

PLATE IV

MONK ILLUMINATING

But inability and unwillingness to read are contemplated:

but if any one be so negligent and lazy that he will not or can not read, some task shall be imposed upon him which he can do; so that he be not idle.

When St Dunstan wrote his *Concordia* in the tenth century, the monks were evidently reading daily, and the same remark applies to the period of Lanfranc's *Statutes*. Some abbeys had of course a greater reputation than others. Symon, Abbot of St Albans from 1167 to 1183, did much to attract learned men to that abbey. The early part of the thirteenth century was not remarkable for learning, but the coming of the friars did much to stimulate the monks. The Benedictine General Chapter held at Canterbury in 1277 ordained that

in place of manual labour the Abbots shall appoint other occupations for their claustral monks according to their capabilities (namely) study, writing, correcting, illuminating and binding books.

To the early monks we owe without doubt, not only the preservation by copying of many important books, sacred and profane, but some of the most beautiful illuminations the world has ever seen. In Ireland the Book of Kells, now at Trinity College, Dublin, is the most famous. It was called "The Great Gospels of Columba" and dates from the latter half of the seventh century. The Lindisfarne Gospel Book, now in the British Museum, is a little later, and was written on Holy Island "for God and St Cuthbert." It shews

Irish influence, but, on the whole, is founded on late Roman or Byzantine models. It is difficult to imagine anything more magnificent, in colour or design, than this Gospel Book. One page must often have taken months to complete, but time was of little account to a monk who could look forward to years of such regular work. The cost of such a production now would be enormous, even if anyone could be found to undertake it, but, to a monk who was not allowed to own anything, money had little meaning. An artist who need not think of time and money has an enormous advantage over his fellows.

Initial letters were a marked feature of mediaeval manuscripts. In 1489 a monk of Westminster applied to the abbot to be transferred to Wenlock, and he was received at that priory as a celebrated maker of capital letters. To the true monk, however, art was subordinate to spiritual life. The 57th chapter of the Rule says

Artificers, if there are any in the monastery, shall practise with all humility their special arts, if the abbot permit it. But if any one of them becomes inflated with pride on account of knowledge of his art, to the extent that he seems to be conferring something on the monastery: such a one shall be plucked away from that art; and he shall not again return to it unless the abbot perchance again orders him to, he being humiliated.

Bury was celebrated for bookbinding in the fourteenth and fifteenth centuries. Of other arts, embroidery may be mentioned, for which the English nuns were noted in the thirteenth century.

PLATE V

A PAGE OF THE LINDISFARNE GOSPELS

The Cloister

The roll of monastic historians includes such names as the Venerable Bede, Florence of Worcester, and William of Malmesbury. Matthew Paris, a monk of St Albans, was intimate with Henry III. At the Feast of Edward the Confessor in 1247 the king commanded him to come and sit on the step midway between his throne and the altar, and added

I therefore beg you and in begging order you to write a special and full account and record all these proceedings in fair writing indelibly in a book, that the memory of them be not lost by any length of time.

It has been claimed that the study of medicine at St Benedict's abbey of Monte Cassino gave rise to the University of Salerno in the ninth century. On the whole, however, the universities were founded in complete independence of the monasteries. Walter de Merton, the real originator of the collegiate system in 1274, distinctly excluded monks and allowed none of his scholars to take vows. Before the end of the thirteenth century, the English universities had become so important that the monks were obliged to take note of them. In 1283 John Giffard, lord of Brimsfield, founded at Oxford a house for thirteen monks of Gloucester. Other great abbeys built sets of rooms adjoining, and there are considerable traces of "Gloucester Hall" in the modern foundation of Worcester College. In 1290 Durham founded a hall in the same university, where Trinity College now stands. At Cambridge in 1340 a hostel, afterwards incorporated in

9

Trinity Hall, was founded for Ely monks. Croyland in 1428 sent monks to their own hostel, afterwards Buckingham College, and still evident in the main court of Magdalene College. The Benedictine General Chapter of 1290 ordered one monk out of twenty to go to the university. Three quarters went to Oxford and one quarter to Cambridge. Novices were sometimes sent as well as monks. At Durham

yf the maister dyd se that any of theme weare apte to lernyng, and dyd applie his booke, and had a pregnant wyt withall, then the maister dyd lett the Prior have intellygence. Then, streighte way after, he was sent to Oxforde to schoole, and there dyd lerne to study Devinity.

The Cistercians were at first not a literary Order, and the *Carta Caritatis* laid it down that no abbot or monk was to make a book without the consent of the General Chapter. Afterwards, however, they became like other Orders, and in 1437 Archbishop Chichele founded St Bernard's College for them at Oxford: St John's College is now on its site.

The regular canons had no colleges of their own in either university, but they owned at Oxford the important Priory of St Frideswide (now the Cathedral) and at Cambridge the Priory of Barnwell. At the latter we know that canons from other houses were received to study, but the plan did not work well.

All through the Middle Ages the monasteries trained their own novices. At first they educated also a number of boys who had no intention of becoming monks. Gradually this plan ceased as grammar schools were founded. It should be remembered, however, that some of these were due to the monks. In 1198 Abbot Sampson built and endowed the public school at Bury. The Abbots of Evesham gave £10 a year and board and lodging in the monastery to the schoolmaster of the free school. The secular clergy were often educated in such monastic schools.

CHAPTER II

The Eastern Claustral Buildings

THE south transept of the church is the north-eastern termination of the east walk of the cloister. Immediately south of it, in the normal Cistercian plan, is the library. In most other Orders the position is occupied by the slype, though this may be placed further south. The slype was a passage leading from the cloister to the cemetery. It was also the inner parlour, or talking place. At one time conversation was forbidden in the cloister, but Lanfranc allowed it at certain times and on certain days: at other times the monks had to obtain leave to go to the parlour. At St Augustine's, Canterbury, there was a restriction as to subjects of talk in the cloister:

Let no one dare to ask about the gossip of the world nor tell it, nor speak of trifles or frivolous subjects apt to cause laughter.

At Durham, just before the Dissolution, the parlour was also "a place for marchaunts to utter ther waires." This reveals a sad declension from monastic fervour. Even if we suppose the merchants came to the parlour through the cemetery, and not through the private cloister, we wonder at their being allowed at all, when, according to the Rule, a monk had of his own "absolutely not anything: neither a book, nor tablets, nor a pen—nothing at all." As early as the end of the twelfth

PLATE VI

FURNESS.   NORTH-EAST CORNER OF THE CLOISTER

century we find private property being owned by individual monks. The custom was winked at, though Abbot Sampson made some attempt to stop it. *The Rites of Durham* speaks of wages, as much as twenty shillings, being given in the year "to find themselves apparel." This was no doubt found to be a more convenient plan than a strict application of the Rule.

Next to the parlour was the chapter house, an important building in position, form and purpose. It is absent from the earliest Benedictine plan we have, the abbey of St Gall in Switzerland, dating from the early ninth century. It occurs in the Norman drawing of Canterbury and is universal all through the Middle Ages, leading out of the east walk of the cloister. It was usually rectangular, but may be apsidal, as at Durham, Norwich, Rievaulx, and Shrewsbury. It was octagonal at Westminster and Bolton, and twelve-sided at Dore. At Worcester it is circular inside with a central vaulting pillar. In a Cistercian house it often had three alleys: at Rievaulx there are five. At the west end are one or more arches, or an arch and two windows. Sometimes there was a vestibule, as at Westminster, Chester, and Bristol.

The chapter house is often richly ornamented, as at Bristol and Wenlock, and rivals the church in beauty. It was often copied in secular churches, but used less frequently. York, Lincoln, Wells, Salisbury, Southwell have beautiful chapter houses, but were not monastic.

13

The Home of the Monk

The chief use of the chapter house was for the meeting of the whole convent, usually held early in the morning. In 1334, Benedict XII laid it down that there was to be a daily meeting wherever six monks were congregated. At this meeting the brethren sat in order of seniority, the youngest at the west end. The Rule was read through, in a Benedictine house, three times in a year, and in a Cistercian house once. The regular canons no doubt read their Rule also, but it was not comparable in importance with the Benedictine: their chapter meeting took place at least weekly. Then there were commemorations of benefactors, deceased abbots and priors, and martyrs of the Order: *obits* from other houses were read. The whole ended with *Requiescant in pace*. Other things were read from a lectern, remains of which can be seen at Cleeve: certain psalms and collects, letters from the king or the bishop. A sermon might be preached, or the precentor might go through the services for the next twenty-four hours. The notice board of duties would be given out, each monk rising and bowing when his name was mentioned. The business of the monastery was discussed, as provided in the 3rd chapter of the Rule:

As often as anything especial is to be done in the monastery, the abbot shall call together the whole congregation, and shall himself explain the question at issue. And, having heard the advice of the brethren, he shall think it over by himself, and shall do what he considers most advantageous. And for this reason, moreover, we have said that all ought to be called to take counsel: because often it is to a younger person that God reveals what is best.

14

PLATE VII

BRISTOL. INTERIOR OF THE CHAPTER HOUSE,
LOOKING WEST

The Eastern Claustral Buildings

In the chapter house the discipline of the monastery was administered. There was open confession of fault, and in some cases the brethren accused one another! Punishments varied in different houses. At St Augustine's, Canterbury, the following were in force for light faults: separation from the common table, meals to be three hours late, a lower place in chapter and quire, prohibition of celebrating mass and reading in public, reception at Holy Communion forbidden. For graver faults there might be ordered: perpetual silence in quire and elsewhere, bread and water only on two days of the week, the last place in the community, or, most disgraceful of all, prostration at the door of the church so that every monk going into quire had to step over the culprit's body. An actual example may be quoted, from the Premonstratensian house of Langdon: John Boston was brought before the Visitor for not rising to matins, and was ordered bread and water only every Friday till Christmas.

Corporal punishment was common till quite modern times, for grown men as well as boys, and it was often ordered in the monastery. The instrument might be a thick rod, or several thin rods together. In 1336 Benedict XII ordered, for illicit absence from a monastery, severe beating with a *ferula*. Two provisions sometimes mollified the severity of the punishment, one that young men must not do the beating, and the other revealed in the Customary of St Augustine's, Canterbury:

15

While corporal discipline of this kind is being inflicted upon
a brother all the rest sit with bowed and covered head, and with
kind and brotherly affection should have compassion on him.

A prison was sometimes provided in a monastic
gate-house. At Durham the prison "for all such
light offences as was done emonges themselves" still
remains, south of the chapter house. West of the
claustral buildings can still be seen

a strong prysonne call the LYNGHOUSE, the which was ordeyned
for all such as weare greate offenders, as yf any of the Monnckes
had bene taiken with any felony, or in any adulterie, he should
have syttin ther in prisone for the space of one hole yere, in
cheynes, without any company except the master of the Fermery
who did let downe there meate thorowgh a trap dour in a corde,
being a great distance from them.

If a brother did not amend after being often rebuked
for a fault, the Rule prescribed that

the abbot shall act as a wise physician. If he have applied the
fomentations, the ointments of exhortation, the medicaments of
the Divine Scriptures; if he have proceeded to the last blasting of
excommunication, or to blows with rods, and if he see that his
efforts avail nothing: let him also—what is greater—call in the
prayer of himself and all the brothers for him: that God who can
do all things may work a cure upon an infirm brother. But if he
be not healed even in this way, then at last the abbot may use
the pruning knife...lest one diseased sheep contaminate the
whole flock.

The chapter house was sometimes used for secular
purposes, as at Westminster, and at Bury, where, according to Jocelyn, a public meeting of burgesses was
held. The *confratres* were received there, honorary
members to be carefully distinguished from the lay
brethren. William I was a confrater of Cluny and

Battle, Henry VI of Croyland, Wolsey of Evesham, More of Christ Church, Canterbury. There were obvious material advantages in having powerful men attached to the community, but there were disadvantages also. They might have to be entertained at great expense, and favours asked by them would be difficult to refuse.

South of the chapter house was the *calefactorium* or warming house, often called the common house. It was the one place in the whole monastery where the monks were allowed a fire, at which to warm themselves. They must, on wintry days, have eagerly watched for permission to retire to it from the cold cloister. Sitting round the fire it was natural that their tongues should be loosed, and, as we learn from the chronicle of Jocelyn of Brakelond, the conversation was not always profitable. The Rule was very plain on this point:

> Scurrilities...or idle words and those exciting laughter, we condemn in all places with a lasting prohibition: nor do we permit a disciple to open his mouth for such sayings.

Often there was no fireplace in a common house, a brazier of charcoal being used, the smoke escaping as best it could, which was the custom in large domestic halls.

In the Cistercian Order the *calefactorium* led out of the south walk and not the east, and had two large fireplaces. The vaulted hall out of the east walk was, however, not omitted, and there has been much discussion as to its purpose. At Furness and Jervaulx there were open arches at the south, and it has been supposed that the hall was used for some manual labour which specially needed fresh air: it was sometimes cut up into separate chambers.

The upper floor of the eastern range was nearly always the *dormitorium* or dorter, and was approached from the cloister by a stone staircase out of the east walk, or occasionally out of the south. In addition to this there might be another staircase coming straight down into the south transept of the church. The finest remaining is at Hexham, a house of regular canons, but the night staircase is most common in Cistercian abbeys.

The dorter is generally ruined, but good examples remain at Cleeve and Valle Crucis, in the latter case with the unauthorized addition of a fireplace. At Durham the dorter was over the western range and is now the cathedral library. At Gloucester, Winchester, and Worcester it ran east and west, in the last case west of the cloister. At St Augustine's, Canterbury, hay was put on the floor and the beds were of straw, renewed every year. Matthew Paris tells us that at St Albans the beds were of oak. According to the Rule, all the "trappings" necessary were a mat, a woollen covering, a woollen cloth under the pillow, and the pillow itself. It was entirely against the Rule for monks to have separate cells. If possible they were all to sleep in one place, the beds of the younger being interspersed among those of the elder.

PLATE VIII

FOUNTAINS. SOUTH-EAST CORNER OF THE CLOISTER

And when they rise for the service of God, they shall exhort each other mutually with moderation, on account of the excuses that those who are sleepy are inclined to make.

As late as 1336, Benedict XII laid it down that the monks were not to sleep in separate chambers. At Durham, however, and no doubt in other abbeys also, cubicles were introduced before the Dissolution:

every Monncke having a litle chamber of wainscott, verie close, severall, by themselves, and ther wyndowes towardes the Cloyster, every wyndowe servinge for one Chambre, by reasonne the particion betwixt every chamber was close wainscotted one from another, and in every of there wyndowes a deske to supporte there bookes for there studdie.

This last arrangement is a reflection of the Rule, which provided, as was the custom in Italy, for an afternoon siesta, but laid it down that

he that wishes to read may so read to himself that he do not disturb another.

It is not to be supposed that the dorter was the normal place for study. Seven or eight o'clock was the time for retirement, and two o'clock in the morning for rising. The first service, that of matins, was so long that Lanfranc provided for a rest after it was over. Matins began at midnight at Durham, and also at St Augustine's, Canterbury. Probably in both rest was allowed afterwards. Nothing is said in the *Rites* about an afternoon sleep. After dinner the monks went

streight into the Scentorie garth, wher all the Monnks was buried, and thei did stand all bair-heade, a certain longe space, praieng amongs the toumbes and throwghes for there brethren soules

being buryed there, and, when they hadd done there prayers, then
they did returne to the Cloyster, and there did studie there
bookes, until iij of the clocke that they went to evensong.

The 55th chapter of the Rule speaks at length of the
clothing allowed to the monks. It was to be inexpensive
and simple, but not too much mended, as the old
clothes were given to the poor. At Barnwell the summer allowance was given out at Easter: a surplice,
shirt, three pairs of linen breeches, one pair of summer
hose of soft leather, one pair of leather shoes, one pair
of gaiters of serge or canvas, a cope of frieze without
fur. On St Michael's day, or rather before, the winter
clothing was begun: one new tunic of woollen or one
cassock of lambskin, one pair of felt boots, one pair of
woollen gaiters, two pairs of woollen shoes, a black
lambskin to mend the fur hood of the cope.

The reredorter, or *necessarium*, always adjoined the
dorter. At Christ Church, Canterbury, it was called, as
a nickname, the *tertium dormitorium*, the dorter there
consisting of two large rooms. Care had to be taken
of the drainage; indeed the proximity of the river
dictated the unusual position of the dorter at Durham
and Worcester. Sometimes, as at Castleacre, a stream
was diverted to pass below the reredorter. The
drainage arrangements were much better than might
be expected. The main drain was often quite a large
tunnel, and has probably given rise to the frequent
rumours of underground passages connecting an abbey
with buildings some way off.

The Eastern Claustral Buildings

One other building over the eastern range should be mentioned, the treasury, which was sometimes placed over the eastern bay of the chapter house: the part west of it may have been a passage, for the actual dorter sometimes began south of the chapter house. Such a position for the treasury was strong and difficult of access. At Durham the treasury was on the ground floor of the western range, and in it

there besst Evidennces and the Chapter seale ar keapt....Within the said treasury was a strong iron grate...so fast as not to be broken, and in the midst of the grate a door of iron...with a strong lock upon it and two great shuts of iron for the said door. ...Within this treasury were...also the Evidences of several gentlemen's lands in the country, who thought them safer there than in their own custody.

CHAPTER III

𝕮𝖍𝖊 𝕾𝖔𝖚𝖙𝖍𝖊𝖗𝖓 𝕮𝖑𝖆𝖚𝖘𝖙𝖗𝖆𝖑 𝕭𝖚𝖎𝖑𝖉𝖎𝖓𝖌𝖘

LEADING out of the walk opposite the church was invariably the large dining hall called the *refectorium*. It is shewn in the Norman drawing of Canterbury, and indeed in the much earlier plan of St Gall. The Latin word is generally anglicized to refectory, but the old English name is frater, frater house, or fratry. In most abbeys the axis was parallel with that of the church, and windows were placed high up over the cloister roof. In the Cistercian Order the normal position was north and south, and most of the windows could come lower down, but in a few cases, such as Sibton and Merevale, the frater ran east and west: at Cleeve it was rebuilt in this form in the fifteenth century, the original frater having been north and south. In the houses of regular canons the hall was usually on an upper floor, with cellars below, and the same plan obtains in some Benedictine abbeys. At Fountains the frater was 110 ft. long by 46 ft. wide: at Bury it was no less than 171 ft. long. The arrangement of the hall was similar to that at colleges in Oxford and Cambridge. At the high table, on a dais, would sit the chief officers and perhaps monastic guests. At the lower tables, at right angles to the dais, would be the ordinary brethren, the youngest near the door. At St

PLATE IX

FOUNTAINS.   SOUTH-WEST CORNER OF THE FRATER

Albans there were no less than fifteen steps up to the abbot's table.

No fire was allowed in the frater, though on the cold island of Lindisfarne there was evidently a brazier in the centre.

At the beginning of a meal the *skilla* or gong was struck by the president, grace being said by the precentor or succentor. At Barnwell quite a short service was held. Dishes were handed first to the superior, then to the seniors, and then to the juniors. The Customaries provide very quaint evidence of the habits of the frater. At St Augustine's, Canterbury, no waiter was

allowed to carry three dishes at once. The refectory being the common dining-hall, no singularity in eating or drinking is allowed. No noise to be made; for instance, if there are nuts, they are not to be cracked with the teeth, but a monk is privately to open them with his knife.... Should he spill anything, he has to go and do penance in the middle of the refectory if strangers are not present. He is not to make signs across the refectory, not to look about or watch what the others are doing; he is not to lean on the table; his tongue and eyes are to be kept in check, and the greatest modesty observed.

At Barnwell we are told that

The servitors are to serve the food quickly and actively, not running or jumping in an unbecoming fashion, and they are to hold the dishes neither too high nor too low, but so that the food may be seen by him who carries it. The dishes are not to be broken, or dirty, or unsuitable, or smeared on the under side. The servitor should use both hands, and carry only a single dish, except when he is serving eggs. If he cannot bring the brethren all they ask for, he ought, nevertheless, to reply to them civilly. ... The brethren ought all to be careful not to wipe their noses, or rub their teeth, on the napkins or table-cloths, nor to staunch blood with them, nor to handle anything that is unclean with them, or cut them with their knives.

In the "Babees Book" for the instruction of novices,

The youthful monk is bidden to wash his hands before his meals, to keep his knife sharp and clean and say his grace.... He is not to seize upon the vegetables, not to use his own spoon in the common dish; not to lean upon the table; not to cut or dirty the table cloth.... Further, he is not to use his knife to carry the gravy to his mouth, but to help others, as only the ill-mannered and clowns take everything for themselves. He is to wipe his knife before he cuts the common cheese, and not to taste first whether it be good enough for him. Finally, his meal ended, he is to clean his knife and cover it with his napkin.

During meals, one of the brethren read from a stone pulpit usually forming a striking architectural feature in the south wall. Three fine examples may be mentioned which still remain: Beaulieu, Chester and Shrewsbury. The staircase was generally in the thickness of the wall. According to the Rule, the weekly reader was solemnly blessed on Sunday: he was not appointed in rotation, but because he could read to edify the hearers. He received a slight refreshment before the reading, and dined afterwards with the weekly cooks and servitors. At Barnwell it is laid down that

The Reader at Table ought not to hurry his reading with the view of reading much, but he should read clearly and distinctly so as to be understood; and when he has found a good and noteworthy passage, he ought to repeat it again and again, that it may be thoroughly understood. He is to correct any mistake he may make at a nod from the President.

The Southern Claustral Buildings

The *Liber Albus* of Bury contains a list of books read in the frater in a cycle of three years: it includes Gregory's *Pastoral*, Jerome, St John's Gospel, Bede, St Benedict's *Vita*, and Gregory on Ezekiel. Recesses often remain in a frater, in which were kept books, as well as plate. According to the Rule, reading also took place after the evening meal, when

one shall read selections or lives of the Fathers, or indeed anything which will edify the hearers. But not the Pentateuch or Kings; for, to weak intellects, it will be of no use at that hour to hear this part of Scripture; but they shall be read at other times.

From Easter to Whitsun dinner was to be at noon and supper just before dark. From then to September 13 dinner on Wednesday and Friday was to be at three o'clock, and this was the daily regulation from September 13 to the beginning of Lent. During Lent dinner was not taken till just before dark. The severity of this order bears rather on the lateness of dinner for a great part of the year than on the fewness of meals, which was the rule in the Middle Ages and still obtains in some countries. The 39th chapter contains full directions as to the food to be eaten and ends with

the eating of the flesh of quadrupeds shall be abstained from altogether by every one, excepting alone the weak and the sick.

In reading of such strict regulations it is natural to enquire how far they were kept. In times of monastic fervour they were certainly taken literally. For example, in the early twelfth century the Cistercians were allowed two dishes of vegetables cooked without grease and never took flesh meat of any kind. A literal interpretation did not exclude fowls and other birds, or fish; though, contrary to modern practice, fish would not be taken on a fast day. It is not surprising that, after a time, it should be questioned whether St Benedict, if legislating for a cold northern climate, would have laid down the same regulations as for Italy, even though he may have regarded his Rule as applying, on the whole, to all countries. In this, as in other matters, the individual abbot would always have in mind a saving clause in the 41st chapter:

he shall so temper and arrange all things, that their souls may be saved on the one hand; and that, on the other, what the brothers do they shall do without any justifiable murmuring.

St Ethelwold in the tenth century permitted, at Abingdon, a dish of stew mixed with meat, and on certain feast days meat puddings. The *Concordia Regularis* recognizes the custom of eating meat and allows pork fat through the winter up to Septuagesima. In 1237 the papal legate congratulated the English abbots on having passed a rule for entire abstinence from flesh meat, but in 1300 a Provincial Chapter, held at Oxford, dispensed with this. In 1334, Benedict XII ordered that no flesh meat was to be taken on Wednesdays and Saturdays, on every day in Advent, and from Septuagesima to Easter: there was no doubt the same regulation for other fast days. In 1421 a decree was passed allowing the eating of meat, for the reason that doctors and experience both teach that a total abstinence from flesh is contrary to nature and hurtful to the system: so were monks to be confined to such diet alone they would become weak and suffer, a thing the Rule neither orders nor desires.

A further relaxation took place in allowing some refreshment in the long intervals between meals. This must have been a real necessity in Lent when the one meal took place more than twelve hours after the monks had risen from bed. The ordinary lunch was called *mixtum* and consisted of bread and wine. At Canterbury and Winchester there are some remains of the turn-table or *rota*, where *mixtum* was placed by the servitor and taken by the brother without communicating with him. At Durham the master of the common house had

to provide for all such spices against Lent as should be comfortable for the said Monnckes for there great austeritie both of fastinge and prayinge...and to have alwaies a hogshead of wyne for the Monnckes...and to provide for fyggs and walnutes against Lent.

The feast of O *Sapientia* was kept in the common house and not in the frater,

a sollemne banquett that the Prior and Covent dyd use at that tyme of the yere onely, when ther banquett was of figs and reysinges, aile and caikes, and therof no superflwitie or excesse, but a scholasticall and moderat congratulacion amonges themselves.

Pittances were extra allowances of food. The word is derived from Old French and is allied to pity. The extra amount was often small, hence the popular use of a "mere pittance." The pittance might be an extra dish of dessert, eggs, fish, or meat given on the anniversary of the donor. One such pittance at Newminster consisted of bread, good ale and salmon. In 1198 there was a serious fire at Bury which damaged the shrine. Abbot Sampson suggested the giving up of pittances for at least a year to repair it, and the convent agreed willingly; but, says Jocelyn,

our resolution was afterwards altered by the sacrist saying that St Edmund could very well repair his shrine without such assistance.

The *pittensarius* had a special lodging at Worcester.

There is therefore a good deal of evidence that meat was increasingly allowed to be eaten, but it is a remarkable fact that the frater was not used for the purpose. In 1298 Archbishop Winchelsey laid it down that meat was not to be eaten in sight of the laity or in the frater. A special hall was built, called at Canterbury the *deportum*, but usually known as the misericorde: it was under the frater at Kirkstall. At Durham it was called the lofte and reached by stairs west of the frater. Just before the Dissolution, the lofte appears to have been used by the monks always, except on St Cuthbert's day, the frater at other times being given over to the novices.

There was always a lavatory near the frater door. It might be a separate octagonal building projecting into the cloister garth, as at Mellifont and Wenlock, but more often it was recessed in the wall of the frater

PLATE X

GLOUCESTER. THE CLOISTER LAVATORY

itself or of the western range. A large number of such recesses are left, as at Haughmond, Kirkham, Norwich. At Fountains there are recesses on either side of the frater doorway. The most complete cloister lavatory still left is at Gloucester. It is an oblong building projecting into the garth and having a trough of stone, which carried away the refuse water after the monks had washed under taps. In the same position at Durham there

was a fair LAVER or CONNDITT, for the Monncks to washe ther hands and faces at, being maid in forme round, covered with lead, and all of marble, saving the verie uttermost walls. Within the which walls you may walke round about the Laver of marble, having many litle cunditts or spouts of brasse, with xxiiij cockes of brasse, rownd about yt, havinge in yt vij faire wyndowes of stone woorke, and in the top of it a faire DOVE-COTTE, covered fynly over above with lead, the workmanship both fyne and costly, as is apparent till this daie. And, adjoyninge to the est syde of the Coundtt dour, ther did hing a bell to geve warning, at a leaven of the clock, for the Monncks to cumme wash and dyne, having ther closetts or almeries on either syde of the Frater House dour keapt alwaies with swete and clene towels, as is aforesaid, to drie ther hands.

There are often signs of the towel rail, but the lavatory at Durham has been taken down and part of it re-erected in the middle of the garth.

In addition to the usual cloister arrangement at Christ Church, Canterbury, there was a lavatory at which the monks washed themselves after leaving the dorter in the morning and before going to matins. It is fortunately still left, a charming little tower, absurdly called the baptistery.

The Home of the Monk

The kitchen, in Cistercian abbeys, opened out of the cloister in the western part of the south walk, but the normal position was the far side of the frater, with which it was always closely connected. At St Gall there was a skew passage between the two, no doubt to keep the smell of the cooking from the dining hall. The kitchen remains at Durham, a fine vaulted structure of the fourteenth century, about 35 ft. square: at Christ Church, Canterbury, it was 47 ft. square. Sometimes, as at Jervaulx, there was a special meat kitchen, vegetables only being cooked in the ordinary kitchen. The pantry, buttery, and scullery were near the kitchen, and often separated from the frater by "screens," as in a large mediaeval domestic hall. The Rule provided for the cooking to be done by the brethren in turn, and for a long time this was carried out in the Cluniac and Cistercian Orders. The tendency, however, was for the cook to be permanent and to become an important official. There is a long account of his duties in the Customary of Barnwell:

The Kitchener ought to know what food and how much should be set before the convent on each day according to ancient allowances.... For gouty persons, and the sick who cannot eat their commons, he ought to provide an alternative.... The Kitchener ought to be careful that food is not served to the convent in vessels that are broken or dirty, and that they are not dirty on the under side, so as to stain the table-cloths. Further, he is to be careful that no food is at any time set before the convent imperfectly cooked, or putrid, or stale; and further, that no excessive noise or clattering take place in the kitchen so long as the convent is in the Frater.

CHAPTER IV

The Western Claustral Buildings

THE largest and finest western range still left in England is at Fountains. The vista of arches is quite a long one, and is often wrongly called the cloisters. This vista, however, is modern, for the range was cut up into several compartments. Of the twenty-two bays, the southern twelve formed the frater of the *conversi*, or lay brethren. There were lay brethren in all the Orders up to the Black Death in 1348–9, when they almost disappeared. The Cistercian *conversi* were of special importance, and special regulations for them are laid down in the *Carta Caritatis*. They were sometimes equal to the monk in social position, but they were not allowed to become monks. It was absolutely forbidden to teach them letters. Ambition was, at all costs, to be rooted out. Like the monk, the lay brother took the three vows of poverty, chastity, and obedience. He had to promise obedience *de bono*, whereas the monk promised only *secundum regulam Sancti Benedicti*. At Waverley about the end of the twelfth century there were 70 monks and 120 *conversi*. At Louth Park a little later there were 66 monks and 150 *conversi*. We do not know the number at Fountains, but the size of the frater indicates a large community. The lay brethren's dorter was over it, and occupied the whole length and breadth of the range: it was reached by a staircase on the west side, and had its own night stairs descending into the church. There was a special infirmary west of the range and a rere-dorter between the two. In several Cistercian abbeys we find between the range and the west walk of the cloister an open space, which has generally been called the "lane." It existed at Citeaux and at Clairvaux, and there are traces of it at Beaulieu, Byland, Kirkstall and Sibton. The reasons for it are unknown; possibly it was connected with some occupation of the *conversi*, the noise of which would be dulled by the west walk of the cloister.

According to the Rule, the monks as well as the lay brethren were to work with their hands. The 48th chapter says:

at fixed times, the brothers ought to be occupied in manual labour; and again, at fixed times, in sacred reading.

The actual hours are prescribed at different periods of the year. Was the order obeyed? Certainly at first: the Cluniacs made a point of it in the tenth century. Before the rise of the Cistercians, however, it had been neglected, and St Bernard consecrated the rule by his own example. It is a remarkable point that the most influential man of his age should have taken his daily turn at ploughing, often falling down faint from his austerities. The Cistercians were great agriculturalists and wool growers, and, to make these things possible, they often had to clear the forests in the lonely spots where they settled. The Benedictine General Chapter of 1277, quoted above, thought that the monks could be better employed than in manual labour, which was done more and more by lay brethren, and finally by paid servants. It is often said that the monks built churches with their own hands. This may have been true in early times, such as at Durham in the eleventh and twelfth centuries, but it was not generally the case. Of course a monk might have a special architectural gift, as Alan de Walsingham had at Ely in the fourteenth century, but the actual manual labour, in monastic as well as secular churches, was generally carried out by the craft of masons.

The western range of a Cistercian abbey has been called the *domus conversorum*. It was that, but it was also the *cellarium*, or place for stores, which often occupied the ground floor of the whole western range in houses of other Orders. The stores were sometimes kept in cellars under the frater. The entrance might be wide, for the convenience of beer barrels, or even large enough, as at Bradsole, to take a horse and cart. The beer was generally poor stuff: in summer it had to be protected from the sun, and in winter the barrels were covered with straw and even warmed by a fire. The cellarer was a very important official: his duties are described in the 31st chapter of the Rule:

As cellarer of the monastery there shall be elected from the congregation one who is wise, mature in character, sober, not given to much eating, not proud, not turbulent, not an upbraider, not tardy, not prodigal, but fearing God: a father, as it were, to the whole congregation....All the utensils of the monastery, and all its substance, he shall look upon as though they were the sacred vessels of the altar. He shall deem nothing worthy of neglect; nor shall he give way to avarice; nor shall he be prodigal or a squanderer of the substance of the monastery.

On the day when this chapter was read at St Augustine's, Canterbury, the cellarer gave a feast to the monks. Some duties were deputed to other officials, such as the sub-cellarer, the fraterer, and the kitchener, but the cellarer was the head of the department of supply. Jocelyn calls him the second father of the monastery and tells us that, at Bury, he held a court to judge thieves and robbers. At Barnwell the cellarer was to attend to everything connected with food, drink, and firing:

Moreover all carriage of goods, whether by land or water, repairs of houses, all purchases of iron, steel, wood, ploughs, and waggons, and all purchases of bacon, stores of salt and dried fish, gowns, wine; together with the entire care of the whole monastery, both inside and out, excepting the duties of the other officers, fall within the province of the Cellarer. On this account he ought frequently to visit the manors, the plough-lands, and the folds; to take cognisance of the stores; to keep a sharp lookout on the character, the acts, and the zeal of the lay brethren, and of all servants placed in charge of manors, lest they should sell stores, corn, wool, make presents, be addicted to squanderings and revellings, or presume to make any innovation without his advice and direction. . . . It is desirable that the Sub-Cellarer should be obliging, of a cheerful countenance, temperate in his answers, courteous to strangers, and of polished manners, so that he may not only not speak harshly himself, but may know how to bear with equanimity the hard words of others, and when he has no substance to distribute, may hand out a gentle reply, for a soft answer turneth away wrath....He ought to be careful over the bread and the drink of the brethren....He may give them warm bread, but it must not be dirty, broken, or burnt, or gnawed by mice....On all principal feasts of first dignity the Cellarer is to provide the convent, for four days, with bread of superior quality, and beer of extra strength.

The cellarer's checker, or office, was in or near the *cellarium*. At Durham it adjoined the kitchen on the west side.

Part of the ground floor of the *cellarium*, generally the bay next the church, was often the outer parlour, where a monk could be visited by his relations. In the Norman drawing of Christ Church, Canterbury, it is shewn as a cloister on the far side of the frater, and called the *locutorium*.

The upper part of the western range in a small house was devoted to guests, but in a large abbey this would be extended westwards or a special house would be built, the *domus hospitum*, which might be quite outside the cloister. In such great institutions there were three classes of guests: the aristocracy, entertained by the abbot or prior; the better class in the guest house; and the poor in the almonry, at or near the gate. The tendency of course was to treat the rich best and to expect a large contribution from them, but the ideal is set forth clearly in the 53rd chapter of the Rule:

All guests who come shall be received as though they were Christ: for He Himself said: "I was a stranger and ye took me in." And to all, fitting honour shall be shown; but, most of all, to servants of the faith and to pilgrims. When, therefore, a guest is announced, the prior or the brothers shall run to meet him, with every office of love. And first they shall pray together.... In the case of all guests arriving or departing: with inclined head, or with prostrating of the whole body upon the ground, Christ, who is also received in them, shall be adored.... Chiefly in the reception of the poor and of pilgrims shall care be most anxiously exhibited: for in them Christ is received the more.

It is one of the finest pictures in literature, and it is finely illustrated by Dauban in the Luxembourg at Paris. The keeping of such a rule was a test of monastic fervour. In times of zeal, such as the Cistercian revival, the ideal might be reached, but in times of laxity thè poor would be regarded as a nuisance. In days when inns were scarce the monasteries would be a great convenience to the traveller. The usual stay was two days and two nights, an extension being allowed for illness. The powerful were apt to plant themselves upon a monastery for a long period. In the time of Henry VIII, we read of a man with wife and seven children arriving and staying for seven years!

At Durham there appears to have been unusual liberality and mixture of classes.

There was a famous house of hospitallitie, called the GESTE HAULE, within the Abbey garth of Durham, on the weste syde, towardes the water, the terrer of the house being master thereof, as one appoynted to geve intertaynment to all staits, both noble, gentle, and what degree so ever that came thether as strangers, ther interteynment not being inferior to any place in Ingland, both for the goodnes of ther diett, the sweete and daintie furneture of there lodgings, and generally all things necessarie for traveillers. And, withall, this interteynment contynewing, not willing or commanding any man to departe, upon his honest and good behavyour. This haule is a goodly brave place, much like unto the body of a Church, with verey fair pillers supporting yt on either

PLATE XI

RECEPTION OF GUEST

syde, and in the mydest of the haule a most large rannge for the fyer.... The victualls, that served the said geists, came from the great Kitching of the Prior, the bread and beare from his pantrie and seller. Yf they weare of honour they weare served as honorably as the Prior himselfe, otherwise according to ther severall callinges.

At Barnwell the hosteller corresponded with the terrer at Durham. He was to have

elegant manners and a respectable bringing-up. By the help of these endowments, in walking, in standing, and in all his movements, he ought neither to do nor to say anything but what sets monastic life in a creditable light; and, if he have no substance to bestow, he may at any rate exhibit a cheerful countenance, and agreeable conversation; for friends are multiplied by agreeable words.... By shewing cheerful hospitality to guests the reputation of the monastery is increased, friendships are multiplied, animosities are blunted, God is honoured, charity is increased, and a plenteous reward in heaven is promised. It is part of the Hosteller's duty to be careful that perfect cleanliness and propriety should be found in his department, namely, to keep clean cloths and clean towels; cups without flaws; spoons of silver; mattresses, blankets, sheets not merely clean but untorn; proper pillows; quilts to cover the beds of full width and length and pleasing to the eyes of those who enter the room; a proper laver of metal; a bason clean both inside and out; in winter a candle and candlesticks; fire that does not smoke; writing materials; clean salt in salt-cellars that have been well scrubbed; food served in porringers that have been well washed and are unbroken; the whole Guest-House kept clear of spiders-webs and dirt, and strewn with rushes underfoot...a sufficient quantity of straw in the beds; keys and locks to the doors, and good bolts on the inside, so as to keep the doors securely closed while the guests are asleep. Further, as in these and all other matters pertaining to his office he ought to love propriety and cleanliness, so ought he to avoid waste, theft, and extravagance.

CHAPTER V

The Abbot's House

THE claustral buildings follow a more or less definite plan and the variations are comparatively unimportant. Outside the cloister there is much more uncertainty, and buildings were placed where convenience dictated.

The guest house has already been dealt with, as it is often part of the western range. The lodging of the head of the monastery, abbot or prior, is also placed sometimes in this position, as at Chester and Westminster. In the Cistercian Order the abbot's house generally adjoins the dorter and is therefore attached to the eastern range. The *Carta Caritatis* orders the abbot to sleep in the dorter, but as early as the twelfth century, as at Kirkstall, the regulation was evaded by joining his sleeping apartment, or even a connecting gallery, to the wall of the dorter. The Cistercian abbot was to live the common life as far as possible, but gradually he became as important and as separate as his Benedictine brother, and his position is reflected in the growing complexity of his house. In this, as in some other respects, the Premonstratensian or white canon corresponded to the Cistercian or white monk, and we notice the same change as time goes on. At Easby, for example, the abbot was provided with a

PLATE XII

WENLOCK. INFIRMARY AND PRIOR'S LODGING

hall, a solar, a bedroom, an oratory, and there are fireplaces. In the Cistercian Order, an extra room or set of rooms seems to have been provided, as at Fountains and Furness, for the visiting abbot, whether of the parent house of Citeaux, or of one of the four daughter houses of La Ferté, Pontigny, Morimond, Clairvaux.

In a large Benedictine abbey, and to some extent an Augustinian, the abbot was frankly a great lord with a large house. The head of a Cluniac monastery was a prior and subject to the Abbot of Cluny, but he sometimes had a grand house all the same, as at Wenlock.

One of the most complete of the great abbots' houses was at Gloucester. From the Dissolution to 1862 it was used as the Bishop's palace, but has now been rebuilt. It was an elaborate structure, not differing greatly from the house of a secular nobleman. At Wenlock, in the thirteenth century, the prior had a beautiful hall south of the dorter, and the solar east of it still remains. In the fifteenth century a splendid camera was added further east, with several chambers and connecting corridors on both floors.

At Durham the bishop corresponded to the abbot and lived in the grand Norman castle north of the cathedral which is now University College. The arrangement of a cathedral and monastery being combined is very uncommon outside England, but it obtained at eight Benedictine houses: Canterbury, Coventry, Durham,

Ely, Norwich, Rochester, Winchester, Worcester. Carlisle was cathedral and Augustinian. At these cathedral priories, the prior, though nominally subject to the bishop, was the acting head of the monastery, and had a great house of his own.

In the 2nd chapter of the Rule of St Benedict there is a beautiful description of what the abbot, or father of the monastery, should be like. Later on, in the 56th chapter, it is laid down that

The table of the abbot shall always be with the guests and pilgrims. As often, however, as guests are lacking, it shall be in his power to summon those of the brothers whom he wishes.

This was all very good, but, like every other regulation, it was liable to abuse. Matthew Paris describes the faults of the abbots of St Albans: for example, Wulsig, the third abbot, was choice in his table, courted the favour of great persons, invited vast numbers of ladies of rank to dine with him. Giraldus Cambrensis tells us that he dined with the Prior of Canterbury and noted sixteen dishes, much sending of dishes from the prior to the monks with ridiculous gesticulation in returning thanks, whispering, loose idle licentious discourse; herbs brought in and not tasted; numerous kinds of fish roasted, boiled, stuffed, fried; eggs; dishes exquisitely cooked with spices; salt meats to provoke appetite; many kinds of wine. Hospitality might very easily degenerate into revelry. Robert de Insula, Bishop of Durham in the thirteenth century, kept two monkeys, and after dinner made

PLATE XIII

DURHAM CATHEDRAL AND CASTLE

them fight for almonds. The household of the Abbot
of St Augustine's, Canterbury, included two chaplains,
a chamberlain, a seneschal, a marshal of the hall, a
carver, a waiter, a pantler, a master of the horse, a cook,
a valet, a cupboard man, a porter, a hall cook and
servant, a messenger, a palfrey man, an almoner. All
of these had their salaries and perquisites and servants
to wait on them.

Ambition was held up to the monk as one of the
greatest vices, but it was very difficult to avoid it,
when any monk might be elected abbot. At first the
bishop of the diocese appointed the abbot, but the
arrangement did not last long. Final episcopal control
remained the rule in Benedictine houses, the only
exempt abbeys in England being St Albans, Westminster, Canterbury (St Augustine's), Bury, and Evesham. Even Glastonbury, though the most ancient,
and at one time taking precedence of other abbeys,
remained subject to the bishop. As early as the eleventh
century exemption from episcopal control was granted
to the Cluniac Order and it followed later to the
Cistercian and Premonstratensian. Augustinian monasteries were not exempt. In most cases, then, the
awkwardness of an *imperium in imperio* was avoided;
but, all through the Middle Ages, the bishops had no
voice in the appointment of abbots. The normal plan
was by the brethren themselves, but, in many cases, the
pope or the king did not allow a free election. This
was especially the case at Christ Church, Canterbury,

where the abbot would be archbishop and primate of all England. There is a deeply interesting account in the Chronicle of Jocelyn of Brakelond of an interregnum at Bury. The brethren chose three to present to the king, and Sampson was chosen, one of the most remarkable abbots of the Middle Ages. As a rule, when an abbey was exempt from episcopal jurisdiction, a journey to Rome had to be undertaken at the expense of the convent, so that the election should be confirmed. The papal fees were heavy. In 1308, Richard de Sudbury, appointed Abbot of Westminster, had to pay 8000 florins. On return to his monastery, the abbot was received with extraordinary pomp. At an early fourteenth century feast, on such an occasion, there were 6000 guests and 3000 dishes; eleven tuns of wine were consumed, 30 oxen, 34 swans, 500 capons, 1000 geese, 200 sucking pigs, 9600 eggs, and 17 rolls of brawn.

The power of an abbot was despotic and it was very difficult to get rid of him when once installed. When he passed the monks got up and bowed: indeed he was treated just like a king. The 49th chapter of the Rule says:

what is done without the permission of the spiritual Father, shall be put down to presumption and vain glory, and not to a monk's credit. Therefore all things are to be done according to the will of the abbot.

Such a precept naturally led to blind submission, and there are stories of a monk watering a dry stick or attempting to remove a huge rock, because of an order, or a supposed order, of his superior. Charlemagne had to restrain the abbots of his day from mutilating monks and putting out their eyes. Unrestrained power has ever been too much for all but the best men. St Benedict saw this and tried to modify it, but by moral considerations only. The ideal was: "he shall strive rather to be loved than feared." Bearing in mind, however, the large number of scandalous cases, it can scarcely be maintained that his system was successful on this point. Occasionally the ideal was almost reached, as in the case of Abbot Sampson, or of William, Abbot of St Albans, described by Matthew Paris:

Whenever he returned from a journey he had all the poor brought to the gate to receive refection. Every day he attended the duties of the Chapter and the greater Mass; present even on private days he stimulated the others by his spirited chanting; and on the greater and simple feasts came to Vespers, and to Compline daily. He assisted indefatigably at Mattins of twelve lessons, by reading the lesson, singing the response, beginning *Te Deum*, standing with those who stood according to their turns, and animating the whole Choir by his example. He was always present mitred in the midst of the Choir at the Mass of Commemoration of the Blessed Virgin, and on principal feasts always celebrated the Mass at the great Altar.... He always attended the unction of the sick, not far from his stall, about the middle of the Choir, and performed the funeral service in his own person. He never professed a novice but at the great Altar; attended all processions (especially those of Sundays), and never anticipated the hour when the Convent was wont to eat. He lent effectual aid to the fabric of the Church, and its buildings and ornaments. He studied books, preached in the Chapter, and was kind to the writers and their masters. Both in doubtful ordinances of the rule, and in divine services, he took the previous advice of his Convent, and even instructed the old, and removed their doubts.

43

The social position of the greater abbots was equal to that of a nobleman: in at least one case, and that a Cistercian house, the abbot bore the title of earl. He often had lands separate from those of the whole convent, and let them out to knights on knights' service. He travelled about with a great retinue, the last Abbot of Glastonbury having a hundred persons in his train. Benedict XII, about 1346, had to lay it down that abbots should not be absent for more than three months in the year and not at Easter. Garments were often sumptuous, even the lay habit sometimes being affected. The political position was also great, an abbot sometimes ruling over large areas with his own courts. The abbots far outnumbered the bishops in the House of Lords. At one time, there were twenty-eight Benedictine abbots, with the prior of Christ Church, Canterbury, twenty-four abbots of other Orders, and only eighteen bishops. Altogether it was a great position, but not always a happy one. Jocelyn states:

I have heard the abbot say, that if he could have been as he was before he became a monk, and could have had five or six marks of rent wherewith he could have been supported in the schools, he never would have been monk or abbot. On another occasion he said with an oath, that if he could have foreseen what and how great a charge it had been to govern the abbey, he would have been master of the almonry, and keeper of the books, rather than abbot and lord.

Abbeys were sometimes held *in commendam*, laymen away from the monastery being appointed and taking the revenues, in return giving their protection. The

PLATE XIV

GLASTONBURY. THE ABBOT'S KITCHEN

system was started in the eighth century, to meet the inroads of the Saracens, but it was terribly abused, especially in France.

Except in the Cluniac Order the second officer of a monastery was generally the prior. A priory, as a rule, was subject to an abbey at a distance, but, in many cases, a priory became independent and was not elevated into an abbey. In all priories the prior was the acting head, and the second officer was the sub-prior, with important duties. At Durham,

The Suppriors chamber was over the Dorter dour, to th' intent to heare that none should stir or go forth. And his office was to goe every nyghte, as a privy watch, before mydnyght and after mydnyght, to every Monnckes chamber, and to caule at his chamber dour upon him by his name, to se that none of them shold be lacking or stolen furth, to goe about any kynde of vice or nowghtynes. Also the Supprior did sett alwaies in the Lofte amongs the Monncks, at meite, at the tables end, as cheefe amonges them, and to se that every mane did use himselfe according to the order that he had taiken him to.

Before the fifteenth century, the sub-prior had a considerable house fitted up for him at the cathedral priory of Christ Church, Canterbury. He had a special house at Worcester, south of the western range. The second officer at Westminster was the prior: at the Dissolution his house included hall, parlour, kitchen, buttery, and garden. A large abbey might have, in addition to the prior and the sub-prior, third and fourth priors, who acted as a kind of domestic police: they were not allowed to rebuke the brethren, but had to report any misdeed to the chapter.

CHAPTER VI

The Infirmary

THE infirmary of a monastery, or, as the old word is, the farmery, was a much more important building than might be supposed. Its position varied, the quietest part of the monastery being chosen: the most usual was beyond the eastern range and connected with the cloister by a passage under the dorter. At Haughmond it was south of the frater; at Easby it was north of the church. At Christ Church, Canterbury, access to the infirmary was given by a cloister, beyond the eastern range, as long as the great cloister. In a large abbey of the twelfth century, the infirmary hall was generally like the nave and aisles of a church; meals were taken in the centre and the beds were placed at the sides. This was the plan at Peterborough as late as the thirteenth century, but it was draughty and uncomfortable. We find that, in many cases, the old halls were retained, stone walls and other partitions being made to form private rooms, and fireplaces added. In other cases the hall was removed and the infirmary rebuilt on a more convenient plan. This was done at Westminster between 1350 and 1392, the new buildings being placed round a cloister. The old chapel was, however, retained, with nave, aisles, and chancel. Ely had the same plan, but the aisled hall there was retained,

PLATE XV

ELY. INFIRMARY ARCHES

with extensions. At Haughmond there is an aisleless hall of the fourteenth century decidedly larger than the frater. At Wenlock a hall without aisles was built beyond the eastern range in the twelfth century: in the fifteenth century a large eastern wing was added, on two floors, including an infirmary chapel and the prior's lodging. At Easby there is a wide arch from the dorter of the infirmary to the chapel, so that sick brethren might join in the services from their beds.

One of the most complete infirmary plans was that of Fountains. Owing to the contracted site it was necessary to build it on tunnels, over 200 ft. long and 10 ft. in width, through which the river Skell was made to flow. The great hall, built between 1220 and 1247, is no less than 170 ft. long and 70 ft. wide. It had aisles, which were gradually cut up into separate rooms. The chapel was east of the hall, but not directly connected with it.

Three classes of men occupied the infirmary. First, the *sempectae*, the monks who had been professed fifty years, and who naturally required in their old age the better food, the greater warmth, and the more personal attention they would receive in the infirmary. Second, the sick, for whom careful provision was made in all the Orders. The Customary of Barnwell speaks of

sick persons who suffer from attacks of fever, tertian or quotidian; intolerable toothaches; sharp gouty spasms; affections of the brain, the eyes, the throat, the spleen, the liver, and pains in divers parts of the body. But, as they can speak and walk, they ought to go to the Warden of the Order, and point out to him the nature of their infirmity. He, pitying them like a mother, will kindly give them leave to enter the Farmery. Should they be unwilling so to do, let him constrain them with maternal solicitude, and commend their cases to the Master of the Farmery. As they cannot take the same food as the rest of the brethren, the Master of the Farmery is to treat them with special indulgence; he ought to consult a physician, and provide them with baths, draughts, electuaries, and all other things conducive to a speedy convalescence....Some, whether asleep or awake, are struck with illness so suddenly that they lose the strength of their limbs in an instant. Such persons are not forced by the Observances in accordance with the Rule to ask leave to go into the Farmery; but, if accidents of this kind occur at meals, in the Cloister, the Quire, or the Dorter, those who are near the person taken ill ought at once, without delay, to come to his assistance, carry him into the Farmery, and commit the care of him to the Master of the Farmery and his servant....The Prelate ought frequently to see one who has been taken ill in this way about the health of his soul and the purity of his conscience, and then by a true confession, sincere repentance, and worthy reception of the Eucharist, confirm him in the way of eternal life. Further, in a spirit of fatherly solicitude, he ought to exhort the Master of the Farmery to be always at hand to wait upon the sick man, that he may want for nothing to relieve his infirmity or his sufferings, for no book or chalice ought to be considered too precious to be given for the life of a brother in this extremity. Those who exhibit these symptoms may eat, drink, talk, and sleep, at whatever hours and as often as they find convenient, for no rule is imposed upon patients of this class.

The third class of men in the infirmary were those who had been bled, an operation which was very common in the Middle Ages and indeed right down to modern times. In a monastery it took place before a good fire in the common house or in the infirmary. Jocelyn tells us that at these private assemblies at bloodletting season the cloister monks were wont alternately to reveal to each other the secrets of the heart and to talk over matters with everyone.

At Ely there was a weekly *minutio* or blood-letting, each monk being bled every seven weeks. The Cistercians were bled four times a year, in February, April, September, and on St John's Day. At Barnwell the black canons were bled every seven weeks, but

those who find it necessary to lose blood every month, or oftener, so that they cannot wait for seven weeks without danger

could obtain special permission. The Premonstratensian canons were bled six times in the year. It is surprising, at first, to learn that the brethren regarded the bleeding season as a holiday, but it generally meant three days in the infirmary, with more generous fare. At Ely, for the week beginning 1 August 1388, the provision for seven *minuti* and eleven other patients in the infirmary included beef, mutton, pork, veal, pullets, capons, salt and fresh fish, eggs, milk, cream, mustard, cheese, spices. At Barnwell,

Whilst the period of bleeding lasts, namely for three days, the Master of the Farmery ought daily to provide them with one good pittance, suitable to their condition, and, at fixed times, with fire and a candle. Further, he is to provide a clean napkin and towels, goblets and spoons, and all utensils that they will require; and he ought to bestow upon them all the comfort and kindness in his power, for those who have been bled ought, during that period, to lead a life of joy and freedom from care, in comfort and happiness. Nor ought they in any way to annoy each other with sarcastic or abusive language. On this account they ought all to be careful to abstain from jeers and evil-speaking,

and also from games of dice and chess, and other games unsuitable to those who lead a religious life, because, beyond all
doubt, they are offensive to God, and frequently give occasion to
strife and contention among those who play at them. No one
therefore ought to do or say anything that can interfere with the
comfort or the repose of those who have been bled.

The *infirmarius*, or master of the infirmary, had his
lodging near the brethren who were placed in his care.
At Wenlock he had a charming camera on two floors
connected by a private staircase: each room had its
cupboards in the wall. At Barnwell we are told that

the Master of the Farmery...ought to be gentle, good tempered,
kind, compassionate to the sick, and willing to gratify their needs
with affectionate sympathy. It should rarely or never happen that
he has not ginger, cinnamon, peony, and the like, ready in his
cupboard, so as to be able to render prompt assistance to the sick
if stricken by a sudden malady...if they cannot sing the canonical
Hours for themselves, he ought to sing them for them, and
frequently, in the spirit of gentleness, repeat to them words of
consolation, of patience, and of hope in God....Further he
should provide in a spirit of fraternal sympathy, a fire on the
hearth, should the state of the weather require it, a candle, a
cresset, and a lamp to burn all night; and everything that is
necessary, useful, and proper.

At one time the monks gave great attention to
medicine. The Norman drawing of Christ Church,
Canterbury, shews a *herbarium* in the garth of the infirmary cloister: the ancestry of the liqueurs of La
Grande Chartreuse is evidently an ancient one. The
physician of a monastery was sometimes a monk and
sometimes not. Jocelyn speaks, at Bury, of "a certain
brother of ours Walter the physician." The barber-
surgeon was an inferior physician. Benedictine monks

had the crown of the head shaved as well as the face. Up to 1266 the brethren at St Augustine's, Canterbury, used to shave one another, but the operation proved to be a painful one when carried out by amateurs, and so secular persons were hired. The shaving took place in the cloister, in winter once in two weeks, in summer twice in three weeks, four barbers attending. The seniors were shaved first, "because in the beginning the razors are sharp and the towels dry."

Were recreations allowed to the monks? Music was of course a necessity in the church services, but, in some cases, it was evidently allowed as a recreation as well. At St Augustine's, Canterbury, we are told that

if it is considered necessary for anyone who is weak and ill, to have his spirit cheered up by the sound of music and harmony, the infirmarian can provide such relaxation. The sick brother is taken into the chapel and the door is shut; then some brother or some honest and private servant can, without offence, play sweetly the music of the harp for his delectation. But great care must be taken lest any sound or melody of this kind should be heard in the infirmary hall or in the cells of the brethren.

Sir William Corvehill, a monk of Wenlock who died soon after the Dissolution,

was excellently & singularly experte in dyvse of the vij libera sciences & especially in geometre, not greatly by speculacon, but by experience; and few or non of handye crafte but that he had a very gud insight in them, as the making of Organs, of a clocke and chimes, an in Kerving, in Masonrie, and weving of Silke, an in peynting; and noe instrumente of musike beyng but that he coulde mende it.

This points to plenty of provision for the more serious side of recreation. How about games? They are not mentioned in the Rule, but some kinds were clearly forbidden. At Durham there was "a garding and a bowlinge allie" for the novices and possibly for the monks as well. At Finchale, a cell of Durham, we read of a "Player Chamber." Hunting was a very common sport in the Middle Ages and it was difficult to prevent a monk from indulging in it. William of Malmesbury, the twelfth-century historian, speaking of Saxon times, says,

> The monks of Canterbury, like all those in England, were hardly different from seculars...They amused themselves with hunting, with falconry, with horse racing; they loved to rattle the dice; they indulged in drink; they wore fine clothes, studied personal appearance, disdained a frugal and quiet life, and had such a retinue of servants that they were more like secular nobles than monks.

We must allow something to Norman exaggeration of Saxon failings, and the period was also before the Cistercian revival. The love of hunting is very strong in the Englishman. Even Abbot Sampson kept a huntsman, though he did not hunt himself. Jocelyn says that the abbot,

> upon the visit of any person of quality, sat with his monks in some walk of the wood, and sometimes saw the coursing of the dogs, but I never saw him taste of the game.

In 1336 Benedict XII forbade hunting and fowling unless they had parks (*vivaria*) or warrens of their own, or a right of sporting in others, in which case it was allowed, so that they did not keep dogs within the precincts or lend their personal presence to hunting.

The Infirmary

The Cistercians were not permitted to keep bears, cranes, peacocks, hunting dogs, or hawks: no monk or *conversus* was to witness *lusores*. Mastiffs were allowed at Jervaulx to chase wolves. Dogs, hawks, and swine were forbidden to the Premonstratensians. At St Augustine's, Canterbury, early in the fourteenth century, it was forbidden under penalties to play at chess or dice, to use bows or slings, or run with poles, or throw stones, big or little, or to be present at fights or duels, or baiting or cock fighting, or to run in the woods, with shout and hounds, in the profane sport of the chase. Belethus, however, late in the twelfth century, tells us that, at carnival time, monks played at ball. The "Feast of Fools" was apparently observed sometimes at monasteries as well as secular establishments. Jocelyn tells us that, at Bury, there were meetings, wrestlings, matches (on one occasion in the churchyard) between the servants of the abbot and the burgesses of the town. Some monks were apparently present, but "stood afar off." The whole thing was stopped by Abbot Sampson.

The infirmary was connected with the last sad rites for the dying. At Durham

The Monncke, so soune as he sickneth, is conveyed, with all his appurtinans or furniture, from his owne chamber in the Dorter to an other in the Fermery, wher he might have both fyre and more convenyent kepinge, for that they were allowed no fyre in the Dorter. And, at such tyme as ytt appeared to them that accompeyned him in his sicknes that he was not lykly to lyve, they sent for the Prior's chaplaine, who staied with him till he yealded the ghoste. Then the barber was sent for, whose

office is to put downe the clothes and baire him, and put on his
feet socks and bowts, and so to wynde hime in his cowle and
habett. Then is he from thence immediatly caryed to a chamber
called the Dead Mane's Chamber in the said Farmery, and there
to remayne till nyght....At nyght ys he removed from the Dead
Manes Chamber into ST ANDREWES CHAPPELL, adjoyning to the
said chamber and Fermery, there to remayne till eight of the
clock in the mornynge, the said chappell being a place onely
ordeyned for sollemne devocion. The nyght before there
funeralles in this maner, two Monncks, either in kinred or
kyndness the nerest unto him, were appoynted by the Prior to be
speciall murners, syttinge all nyghte on ther kneys at the dead
corsses feet. Then were the chyldren of th' Aumery sitting on
there knees in stalls, of eyther syd the corpes, appoynted to read
David's spalter all nyght over, incessantly, till the said hour of
eight a clock in the morning, at which tyme the corse was
conveyed to the Chapter house, where the Prior and the hole
Covent did meat hime, and there did say there dergie and
devotion...the dead corpes was caryed by the Monnckes from
the Chapter house thorowgh the PARLER...into the Sentuarie
Garth, where he was buryed, and a chalice of wax laid upon his
brest with hime; having his blew bedd houlden over his grave
by iiij Monncks during his funerall, which bedd is dew to the
barber for his dewtie aforesaide and the making of his grave.

The customs at death varied in different Orders and
different monasteries. In early times ashes were strewn
on the floor, covered by a hair cloth, on to which the
dying man was gently lifted. Later on the more humane
practice was adopted of putting the ashes and sackcloth on the bed. St Martin told his disciples that
Christians should die on sackcloth and ashes. At
Glastonbury a portable altar of sapphire was used at
the bedside. At St Augustine's, Canterbury, office was
said for the departed during thirty days, doles were
made to the poor on his behalf, each priest in the

monastery said ten masses and others ten psalters, and his name was sent to all monasteries of all Orders in Great Britain.

In early times the more important monks were buried in the chapter house or in the east walk of the cloister, and later on in the church. The large majority were buried in the cemetery, which was nearly always east of the chapter house and south of the church: the cloister garth was not used for the purpose as is commonly supposed. After a lapse of time the bones were collected and placed in a charnel house, or bone hole. This was in the form of a crypt, with a chapel over. The crypt at Worcester, on the north side of the church, was 58 ft. long by 22 ft. wide and 14 ft. high. There were four, and later six, chaplains, one of them being *magister*, who lived together in a house west of the chapel.

CHAPTER VII

Outbuildings

THE situation of monasteries varied very much. It is often said that the Benedictines chose hills, but this is by no means always the case. In England some of the oldest abbeys, not Benedictine in the narrowest sense, were refounded by them. The Cistercians often chose valleys far removed from the haunts of men. In all Orders there was a tendency to place a monastery near a river for the convenience of drainage. The precinct was often very large, at Glastonbury 60 acres, at Fountains 90 acres, at Jervaulx 100 acres. The reason for this was that the monastery had to be self-sufficient. The 66th chapter of the Rule says:

A monastery, moreover, if it can be done, ought so to be arranged that everything necessary,—that is, water, a mill, a garden, a bakery,—may be made use of, and different arts be carried on, within the monastery; so that there shall be no need for the monks to wander about outside. For this is not at all good for their souls.

The gateway was often a fine architectural structure, and a number of them remain. There were generally two doorways, the smaller one being used as a rule. Over the gateway, or adjoining it, was a room for the porter, whose duties are laid down in the 66th chapter; he was to be

a wise old man who shall know how to receive a reply and to return one; whose ripeness of age will not permit him to trifle.

PLATE XVI

BATTLE. THE GREAT GATEWAY

At Bury the porter was not a monk. The prison was sometimes in the gateway.

There was sometimes a chapel in the gate-house. In the Cistercian Order a *capella extra portas* had to be provided: it was no doubt used by lay folk, the monastery often being far away from a parish church. There are ruins of this chapel near the gateway at Fountains and Furness, and documentary evidence remains of its existence at Byland and Meaux. At Kirkstead it is complete, and it is used at Coggeshall, Tilty, and Rievaulx. At Croxden it was destroyed in 1884. The most important chapel of this kind is at Merevale and is now used as a parish church. It was built in the thirteenth century, but aisles were added at a later date to the eastern part. In 1361 the Bishop of Lichfield granted a commission to Thomas de Leycester, monk of Merevale, to be penitentiary for pilgrims to the chapel of the Blessed Virgin Mary by the gate of the monastery. The Bishop had been informed that large numbers of pilgrims of both sexes came to the chapel, and, by reason of the crush and various diseases prevalent, many were brought to the point of death. Special powers were therefore given to the penitentiary to absolve those in extremity.

At or near the gateway, in a large abbey, was the almonry, where the poorest class of traveller was lodged and where distribution of food to the needy of the district took place. The fine Norman staircase, which still remains at Christ Church, Canterbury, led to a large hall for the entertainment of the poor. Sometimes children or aged women were permanently housed in the almonry, as at Durham. At Glastonbury, Leland tells us, Abbot Bere (1492 to 1524)

made an Almose House in the north part of the Abby for vij or x poor wymen with a Chapel.

Jocelyn says that the almonry at Bury, formerly of wood, was rebuilt in stone by Abbot Sampson. There is a charming description of the *elemosinarius* in the Customary of Barnwell:

The Almoner ought to be kind, compassionate, and God-fearing. He ought also to be discreet, and careful in making his apportionments. He ought to endow with a more copious largess pilgrims, palmers, chaplains, beggars, lepers. Old men, and those who are decrepid, lame, and blind, or who are confined to their beds, he ought frequently to visit, and give them suitable relief. Those who in former days have been rich, and have come to poverty, and are perhaps ashamed to sit down among the rest, he will assemble separately, that he may distribute his bounty to them with greater privacy. He ought to submit with calmness to the loud-voiced importunity of the poor, and help all needy petitioners as far as he is able. If, however, he have not the wherewithal, he ought to answer them with words of patience and moderation; he ought not to strike or hurt, or even abuse or upbraid anyone, always remembering that they are made in the image of God, and redeemed by the price of the blood of Christ. When, therefore, he sees anyone naked, let him clothe him; when he hears of anyone being hungry, or thirsty, or a stranger, or sick, or in prison, let him as far as possible, comfort him with works of piety and pity....Moreover the Almoner ought to have trustworthy servants who will in no wise cheat him in the collection and distribution of remnants—namely by covertly sending them to their laundresses, their shoemakers, and their friends, without his leave or order....To the Almoner pertain the remnants of the Frater, the Prior's chamber, the Farmery and the Guest-House.... According to ancient usage the Almoner is to supervise the letter-carriers, and to receive from them briefs of the brethren who die, which he will hang together on the string of the martyrology.... For the collection of remnants the Almoner ought to keep baskets, porringers, and various vessels, lest through carelessness the vegetables should get mixed with heavy food. He is to take care that his vessels be neither broken nor cracked, for, when vessels are in this condition, liquids may get lost.... Wherefore the Almoner ought to be gentle and kind to the poor, for in them he is ministering to the Lord Jesus Christ. On this account he ought never, or seldom, to be without a stock of socks, linen and woollen cloths, and other necessaries of life; so that if by chance Christ Himself should at some time appear in the guise of a naked or a poor man, He need not go away empty without a gift.

Once through the gate, a large court opens out with the church beyond, but sometimes there was an inner gate before it was reached. The menial offices were in the outer part. At St Gall, early in the ninth century, there were workshops, mills, a factory, a threshing-floor, a kiln, stables, cowsheds, goatsheds, pigsties, sheepfolds, hen and duck houses, poultry keeper's house.

At Christ Church, Canterbury, the *balnearium* or bath-house was some distance east of the cloister. The Rule lays it down that

The use of baths shall be offered to the sick as often as it is necessary: to the healthy, and especially to youths, it shall not be so readily conceded.

At the Benedictine abbey of St Augustine's, Canterbury, it is stated, early in the fourteenth century, that formerly four baths a year were allowed, but at that

time only two. The Augustinian Rule, as observed at
Barnwell, states that

a bath should be by no means refused to a body when compelled
thereto by the needs of ill health. Let it be taken without
grumbling when ordered by a physician, so that, even though
a brother be unwilling, that which ought to be done for health
may be done at the order of him who is set over you. Should
he wish for one, however, when not advantageous, his desire
is not to be gratified. Sometimes, what gives pleasure is thought
to do good, even though it may do harm.

Bathing was of course one of the chief luxuries of
the Roman Empire, and the long-continued prohibition
of frequent baths in the monasteries must be traced to
a reaction against it.

The *granarium* or barn, the *pistrinum* or bakehouse,
the *bracinum* or brew-house, were ordinary necessities.
At Glastonbury a barn remains 85 ft. by 25 ft., with
porches projecting 20 ft. further. An important official
at Durham was the Master of the Garners,

where all there wheat and other corne did lye. His office was to
receyve all the whet that came, and all the malte corne, and to
make accompte what malt was spente in the weeke, and what
malt corne was delyvered to the kylne, and what was receyved
from the kylne, and howe moch was spente in the house.

The monastic mill, sometimes still used, was an
important source of revenue, fees for its use being paid
by people in the neighbourhood. There was a garden,
and often a *plumbarium* or dovecot. At Durham,

The Chamberlaynes Checker was...nyghe to the Abbey gaites.
His office was to provyde for stammyne, otherwaies called
lyncye wonncye, for sheetes, and for sheirtes, for the Novices,
and the Monnckes to weare, for they dyd never weare any

lynynge, and he had a tailler wourkinge daily, makinge socks of white wollen clothe, both hole sockes and halfe socks, and makinge shertes and sheetes of lyncye wonncey, in a shop underneth the sayde checker, which tailler was one of the servauntes of the House.

At Barnwell linen was allowed: the chamberlain had

to provide a laundress of good character and good reputation to wash the garments of the convent. She must be able properly to mend and wash all the linen of the brethren, namely, surplices, rochets, sheets, shirts, and drawers. The linen ought to be washed once a fortnight in summer, and once in three weeks in winter. The Chamberlain is both to give it out to the laundress, and receive it back again, with tallies. If any articles are missing through the carelessness of the laundress she is herself to make them good out of her wages. Moreover, the Chamberlain ought to provide a servant, who shall be fit for his place, trustworthy, sober, unassuming, secret, not talkative, drunken, or lying. He is to know how to shape in due form brethren's woollen and linen garments, which are to be neither too sumptuous nor too sordid. These the servant of the Tailery is to shape in such a way that they be not too long, too short, hanging down unevenly, badly cut, or in any way arranged contrary to usage or so as to attract attention, but, having regard to the stature of each brother, such as fit him properly and according to usage.

The chamberlain also had

to provide warm water for the shaving of the convent, and soap for washing their heads. He is to provide soap for the baths of the brethren, if it be asked for.

The water supply of a monastery was generally excellent, even as early as the twelfth century. The Norman drawing of Christ Church, Canterbury, shews the state of things about 1165 in that great cathedral priory. Up to that time there were wells in the infirmary cloister, and in the cemetery on the opposite side of the church, the latter probably being used by the inhabitants of the city. The new system was much more scientific, and reached a much higher standard than most people would suppose to have been possible at that time. The source was some distance outside the north wall of the city. The water was taken first to a tower, and then through a field, a vineyard, an orchard; the corn, vines, and apple trees being shewn in the drawing. It then passed under the wall of the city, the wall of the monastery, and to the lavatories, to fish-ponds, the cisterns, the bath-house, the kitchen and other offices. Before it reached the city it passed through no less than five filtering tanks, so contrived that they could be easily washed out. At the various places where the water was available it could be drawn out by a stop-cock, but it would have been too risky to allow this in the lay people's cemetery, where a pedestal was fixed to enable the water to be taken out by dipping a pail into it.

As a rule there were two water supplies, as at Gloucester, one for drinking and washing, and one for flushing the drains and the mill. At Westminster a supply came from a spring south of the Serpentine.

Canals received the attention of the monks as well as water supplies. At Rievaulx a canal was made in 1142–1146, and a second about 1160 because the old one had an awkward overflow. A third one was added in 1193–1203 to serve the new quarry. The fish-ponds were an important part of the monastic economy, and were generally provided even if there was a river near.

CHAPTER VIII

The Church

A MEDIAEVAL church of the first rank is one of the greatest things the world has ever seen. This, however, is as true of a secular as of a monastic church, and it would be a futile task to compare, from the point of view of grandeur, the secular Salisbury, Wells, Exeter, Lichfield, Lincoln, York, with the monastic Canterbury, Winchester, Worcester, Ely, Norwich, Durham. On the whole the former have been more rebuilt than the latter. Of no secular church of the first rank can it be said that it remains substantially what it was in Norman times, but, to a great extent, Winchester, Norwich, Durham still date from the eleventh or twelfth century. A discussion of the reasons which led to the erection of all these great churches would be a lengthy one. Motives were mixed, as in so many other things, and there can be no doubt that local rivalry and superstition played their part. There can be no question, however, that the ideal set before the builders was a great house for the glory of God. The population of the neighbourhood had little to do with the problem: it has never been possible to fill with local people some of the parish churches of Norfolk villages. This is even more true of the church of a great monastery. Much, if not all, of the building was reserved for the monks, who may never have reached a hundred in number. In a monastic plan the church sometimes seems as large as all the other buildings put together.

We have seen that the cloister was the centre of the monastic life, but the church had the place of honour, and more time was spent there than anywhere else. The Rule orders that seven times in the day the monks should praise God. Nine services were held, in two cases services immediately following each other. The first was Matins, beginning two hours after midnight and lasting from one and a half to two hours. We cannot be surprised to hear that Lanfranc ordered the prior to go round with a dark lantern and see if any monk was asleep, an even more necessary precaution when the hour of Matins was altered to midnight. St Benedict prescribed meditation in the church after the service, but Lanfranc introduced the custom of returning to bed. Lauds was sung at dawn and was generally followed immediately by Prime. Terce came at nine o'clock, and then High Mass, which is not specifically mentioned in the Rule. Benedict XII in 1336 ordered

Mass to be said not by running it over or shortening it, but gradually and distinctly.

Mass sometimes followed Sext, held rather before the sixth hour. Nones was at three o'clock and Vespers before dusk. Compline came last thing at night, seven o'clock in winter, eight o'clock in summer. In addition to these communal services there were private masses, said by those brethren who were priests at the numerous side altars.

A conventual church was nearly always cruciform, the eastern arm being apsidal or square-ended. Much or all of the arm was taken up by the presbytery, that part of the church where the high altar was placed and where High Mass was celebrated. In the great Benedictine houses the presbytery had aisles, and there was a tendency to add them in the other Orders. At first, however, the Cistercian presbyteries were aisleless, but at Beaulieu, Fountains, and elsewhere, aisles were added later on. Dore was rebuilt with aisles late in the twelfth century. The presbytery was often separated from the aisles by stone walls, in which there were doors.

The high altar was often a grand thing: Jocelyn tells us that at Bury the table was of silver. It was generally reached by three steps, which, at Castleacre, were paved with yellow, black, and green tiles. The reredos often had two doors, as at Durham, Gloucester, Westminster, and Winchester. At Rievaulx we read of

a loft of tymber on the bakside of the high alter with a sele under hit all of wood.

On the south side were the piscina and aumbry as in a secular church. There may be a separate credence recess, a common feature in Cistercian abbeys. On the north side was the Easter sepulchre, the most beautiful example remaining being in a secular church,

The Home of the Monk

Lincoln cathedral. At Durham, on Good Friday, there was a

marvelous solemne service, in the which service time, after the PASSION was sung, two of the eldest Monkes did take a goodly large CRUCIFIX, all of gold, of the picture of our Saviour Christ nailed uppon the crosse, lyinge uppon a velvett cushion, havinge St Cuthbert's armes uppon it all imbroydered with gold, bringinge that betwixt them uppon the said cushion to the lowest greeces in the Quire; and there betwixt them did hold the said picture of our Saviour, sittinge of every side, of that, and then one of the said Monkes did rise and went a pretty way from it, sittinge downe uppon his knees, with his shooes put of, and verye reverently did creepe away uppon his knees unto the said Crosse, and most reverently did kisse it. And after him the other Monke did so likewise, and then they did sitt them downe on every side of the Crosse, and, holdinge it betwixt them, and after that the Prior came forth of his stall, and did sitt him downe of his knees, with his shooes off, and in like sort did creepe also unto the said Crosse, in the mean time all the whole quire singinge an himne. The seruice beinge ended, the two monkes did carrye it to the SEPULCHRE with great reverence, which Sepulchre was sett upp in the morninge, on the north side of the Quire, nigh to the High Altar, before the service time; and there lay it within the said Sepulchre, with great devotion, with another picture of our Saviour Christ, in whose breast they did enclose, with great reverence, the most holy and blessed Sacrament of the Altar, senceinge it and prayinge unto it upon theire knees, a great space, settinge two tapers lighted before it, which tapers did burne unto Easter day in the morninge, that it was taken forth.

There was in the Abbye Church of Duresme verye solemne service uppon Easter Day, betweene three and four of the clocke in the morninge, in honour of the RESURRECTION, where two of the oldest Monkes of the Quire came to the Sepulchre, beinge sett upp upon Good Friday, after the Passion, all covered with red velvett and embrodered with gold, and then did sence it, either Monke with a pair of silver sencers sittinge on theire knees before the Sepulchre. Then they both rising came to the Sepulchre, out of the which, with great devotion and reverence,

66

they tooke a marvelous beautifull IMAGE OF OUR SAVIOUR, representing the resurrection, with a crosse in his hand, in the breast whereof was enclosed in bright christall the holy Sacrament of the Altar, throughe the which christall the Blessed Host was conspicuous to the behoulders. Then, after the elevation of the said picture, carryed by the said two Monkes upon a faire velvett cushion, all embrodered, singinge the anthem of *Christus resurgens*, they brought it to the High Altar, settinge that on the midst therof, whereon it stood, the two Monkes kneelinge on theire knees before the Altar, and senceing it all the time that the rest of the whole quire was in singinge the foresaid anthem of *Christus resurgens*. The which anthem beinge ended, the two Monkes tooke up the cushions and the picture from the Altar, supportinge it betwixt them, proceeding, in procession, from the High Altar to the south Quire dore, where ther was four antient Gentlemen, belonginge to the Prior, appointed to attend theire cominge, holdinge upp a most rich CANNOPYE of purple velvett, tached round about with redd silke and gold fringe; and at everye corner did stand one of theise ancient Gentlemen, to beare it over the said image, with the Holy Sacrament, carried by two Monkes round about the church, the whole quire waitinge upon it with goodly torches and great store of other lights, all singinge, rejoyceinge, and praising God most devoutly, till they came to the High Altar againe, wheron they did place the said image there to remaine untill the Ascension day.

It will be gathered from this extract that there was much pomp in the services of a great Benedictine abbey. Such pomp was forbidden in the Cistercian Order: there was to be no painted glass, no dalmatic, tunicle, or cope, the candlesticks were to be of iron, the crucifix of painted wood, there was to be one chalice only, the one chasuble was to be of fustian or linen and not of silk. In this, as in other respects, the early simplicity in time broke down. For example, fragments of painted glass have been found at Newminster, the elaborate glass in the lady chapel at Lichfield was brought from the Cistercian abbey of Herckenrode in Belgium.

The lady chapel is frequently an addition of the thirteenth century or later. Its usual position is east of the presbytery as at Gloucester, but it may be east of the north transept as at Ely, or elsewhere. At Durham it was at the west end, but for this there was a special reason:

> HUGO, Bishop of Durham, . . . considering the deligence of his predecessors in buylding the Cathedrall Church, which was finished but a fewe yeres before his tyme, no Chappell being then erected to the blessed Virgin Marie, whereunto it should be lawfull for women to have accesse, began to erect a newe peice of woorke at the east end of the said Cathedrall Church, for which worke there weare sundry pillers of marble stone brought from beyonde the seas; but this worke, being browght to a small height, began throwghe great rifts apperinge in the same to fall downe, whereupon it manyfestlye appeared that that worke was not acceptable to God, and holy Saint Cuthbert, especially by reason of the accesse which women weare to have so neare his Ferreter. In consideration wherof the worke was left of, and a newe begun and finished at the west angle of the said Church, wherunto yt was lawfull for women to enter, having no holie place before where they mighte have lawfull accesse unto for there cumforthe and consolation.

The place thus left unoccupied at the east end was more than filled a hundred years later by the chapel of the nine altars, which is also a grand feature in the same position at Fountains. There were five altars here at Dore, and at Rievaulx there were five little chapels not extending beyond the line of the presbytery.

Many of the great abbeys had their shrines, which

PLATE XVII

WESTMINSTER. SHRINE OF EDWARD THE CONFESSOR

were often the chief reason of their fame:—St Thomas at Canterbury, St Edmund at Bury, St Cuthbert at Durham, St Wolstan at Worcester, the Confessor at Westminster. We have a wonderful account of the Christmas of 1433 spent by Henry VI at Bury. Four candles of three pounds weight were always kept burning there, and on festivals twenty-four also of one pound. Jocelyn frequently refers to the shrine and in particular to its miraculous preservation in the fire of 1198. At Durham the shrine of St Cuthbert

was exalted with most curious workmanshipp of fine and costly marble, all limned and guilted with gold, hauinge foure seates or places conuenient under the shrine for the pilgrims or laymen sittinge on theire knees to leane and rest on, in time of theire devout offeringes and fervent prayers to God and holy Saint Cuthbert for his miraculous releife and succour, which beinge never wantinge, made the Shrine to bee so richly invested, that it was estimated to bee one of the most sumptuous monuments in all England; so great were the offerings and jewels that were bestowed uppon it, and no lesse the miracles that were done by it even in theise latter days, as is more patent in the History of the Church at large. At the west end of this Shrine of Saint Cuthbert was a little Altar adjoyned to it for masse to be said on, onely uppon the great and holy feast of Saint Cuthbert's day.

There was a cover to the shrine, and

when the cover of the same was drawinge upp the belles did make such a good sound that itt did stirr all the people's harts that was within the church to repaire unto itt, and to make ther praiers to God and holy Saint Cuthbert, and that the behoulders might see the glourious ornaments thereof.... And on the topp of the cover from end to end was most fyne carved worke, cutt owte with dragons and other beasts, most artificially wrought, and the inside was vernished with a fyne sanguine colour that itt might be more perspicuous to the behoulders.

The feretory was an ornamental iron screen round the shrine. The offerings of pilgrims were a very profitable source of income, and often enabled a church to be rebuilt on a larger scale. For example, the great Augustinian canons' church at Walsingham would not have been possible without the offerings of pilgrims who flocked from all parts of Europe to the celebrated shrine of our Lady there. At Worcester in 1224, we find that the offerings were divided between the bishop and the convent. The *tumbarius*, or shrine keeper, or master of the feretory, had a special house of his own. The usual position for the shrine was east of the high altar: pilgrims would approach by one of the presbytery aisles and return by the other. The necessity of accommodation was one of the chief reasons for the spaciousness of that part of the church.

Relics were much thought of in monastic churches. At Bury possession was claimed of the parings of St Edmund's nails, the knife and boots of St Thomas of Canterbury, and some of the coals which burned St Lawrence. Walsingham was said to have a flask of the Virgin's milk, and a joint of one of St Peter's fingers. Relics were kept in the shrines and in the altars. At Gloucester they were placed in two large recesses beneath the high altar.

The position of the sacristy varied. In the Cistercian Order it was a small chamber leading out of the transept and east of the book closet: later on it was often enlarged. In other Orders it was usually south of the presbytery. In the sacristy the vestments were kept and there was sometimes an oven, as at Castleacre, where the sacramental bread was baked. The sacrist was an important officer, and sometimes had a checker or office separate from the sacristy. He had to provide candles, bread and wine, arrange for bell-ringing, keep the church clean, see that the windows were mended and plumber's work carried out. The number of obedientiaries, or officers, varied in this as in other departments. There might be one or more sub-sacrists. At Bury the master of the vestiary was apparently not the same person as the sacrist or sub-sacrist.

The centre of the church was the choir, or, as it was spelled, quire. In the majority of cases it was placed under the central tower and in the eastern part of the nave; but it might be wholly in the nave, as at Westminster, under the central tower, as at Gloucester, or east of it, as at Durham. In the Cistercian Order the first position was almost invariable, perhaps extending three or four bays into the nave. There was generally a step at the east between the quire and the presbytery. At Bury there was a quire altar, a good deal west of the high altar. The old lectern remains at Peterborough. At Durham,

there was a goodly fine LETTERON of brasse, where they sunge the epistle and the gospell, with a gilt pellican on the height of it, finely gilded, pullinge hir bloud out hir breast to hir young ones, and winges spread abroade, wheron did lye the book that they did singe the epistle and the gosple. It was thought to bee the goodlyest letteron of brasse that was in all this countrye.

71

It was all to bee taken in sunder with wrests, every joynt from other. Also ther was lowe downe in the Quere another LETTORN of brasse, not so curiously wroughte, standinge in the midst against the STALLS, a marveilous faire one, with an EAGLE on the height of it, and hir winges spread a broad, wheron the Monkes did lay theire bookes when they sung theire legends at mattens or at other times of service.

There were screens, of stone or wood, on the north, south, and west sides, against which stalls, covered often with canopies, were placed. The seats, called misericords, turned up, so that partial sitting was possible during the long services. Lanfranc ordered that every other monk was to stand. The order in quire was the opposite to that in the chapter house, the youngest being at the east. The chief officers were at the west facing the high altar, the abbot on the south side. The bishop, in a monastic cathedral, corresponded to the abbot, and his successor still sits in this position at Ely, where there is no throne. Even at Durham, where there is a throne, the bishop has a seat in quire, on the south side. The dean, as successor to the prior, sits on the north, whereas in a secular cathedral the dean, as head of the chapter, sits on the south side.

The quire was closed at the west end by a screen, usually of stone, with one door in the middle. It supported a loft and often took up a complete bay, the whole structure being called the *pulpitum*. From the top, part of the service was sometimes read, and an altar might be placed on it. It was the usual position for the organ, or pair of organs, as the old expression is.

PLATE XVIII

HEXHAM

There were three such pairs at Durham; one on the *pulpitum*, used only on principal festivals, one on the north side of the quire, used when the four doctors of the church were read—Augustine, Ambrose, Gregory, Jerome—and one elsewhere used on ordinary days.

The transepts might be aisleless, but they usually had eastern aisles, and might have western, and also aisles at the ends. The Cistercian arrangement was to have two or three chapels east of each transept, separated from each other by stone walls. From the structural point of view the transepts were valuable as north and south abutments to the central tower. Ritually, they provided room for additional altars, a specially important point in England, where the eastern position of an altar has been almost a matter of faith. Rievaulx abbey is one of the very few cases where an English church in the Middle Ages was built north and south. The transept next the domestic buildings, usually the south, was the more important. It might contain the night stairs to the dorter and have a doorway to the cloister, and a clock was sometimes placed in it: at Wenlock there is a ceremonial lavatory in the west wall. In the transept away from the domestic buildings we sometimes see, especially in the Cistercian Order, an end doorway, the use of which is by no means clear.

Most monastic churches had a central tower, and the larger ones, except in the Cistercian Order, often had two western ones as well. Bury had only one at the west. Sometimes there was a tower quite separate from the church, as in the grand example still remaining at Evesham. The Cistercian tower had to be low, and to contain only one bell, not too large to be rung by one person. At the Dissolution, however, we find that there were five bells at Rievaulx and at Hayles, and seven bells at Byland. At Fountains a lofty tower was built at the end of the north transept late in the fifteenth century or early in the sixteenth.

The monastic nave usually had aisles, especially in Cistercian abbeys and in the greater Benedictine and Cluniac houses. The churches of regular canons frequently had aisles too, but there may be only one, as at Bolton, or none, as at Lilleshall and Shap. In the Benedictine and Augustinian Orders the laity were allowed free access to the altars of the nave, which indeed might be a parish church. In the Cluniac, Cistercian, and Premonstratensian naves there were rarely if ever any parochial rights.

The main object of the nave in the Cistercian order was to provide accommodation for the *conversi*, whose quire took up all the western part. Clear traces of the stone screens against which the stalls were placed may be seen at Tintern and Buildwas. When the *conversi* died out the screens were often taken away, as at Fountains. The nave then became, what it was in other Orders where there were no parochial rights, a grand vestibule to the quire and presbytery and a place for extra altars. The main altar in the centre was the Jesus altar and was placed against the rood-screen, which

PLATE XIX

ST ALBANS. ROOD SCREEN

had two doors in it and was at least one bay west of the *pulpitum*, the intervening space being called the retro-quire. The best example of such a rood-screen still remaining is at St Albans, but in that case it is combined with the *pulpitum*, an arrangement which is also seen in small priories. A few feet west of the rood-screen might be a low fence-screen.

On Sundays before High Mass there was always a grand procession, a custom which prevailed in collegiate and parochial, as well as monastic, churches. The monks left their stalls in quire and went to the high altar, sprinkling it, and passing with the same ceremony to the other altars. They then went through the main church door, south-east of the nave, all round the cloister, through the south-west door, up the nave, making a solemn station before the Rood, through the two doors of the rood-screen, converging to the one door of the *pulpitum*, and so back into quire. Fountains retains the stones in the pavement, which kept the procession regular and provided three places in front for the leaders. The Cistercian procession passed through the domestic buildings as well as the church and cloister. This is no doubt the reason for the absence, in many Cistercian abbeys, of a door from the west walk of the cloister. The procession would pass into the church from the undercroft of the western range or even from the dorter of the *conversi* by a night staircase. Occasionally the west door was also omitted, as at Buildwas: there was no special need for it when lay folk were not admitted. For some reason, which is not clear, there was in several Cistercian churches a *narthex*, or shallow porch, across the west wall.

The north door at Durham was connected with sanctuary, a privilege often abused but pertinaciously claimed by the monks. The author of *The Rites of Durham* says that

the Abey Church, and all the Church yard, and all the circuyte therof, was a SAUNCTUARIE, for all manner of men that had done or commytted any gret offence, as killing of a man in his own defence, or any prisoners had broken out of prison and fled to the said church dore, and knocking and rapping at yt to have yt opened, there was certen men that dyd lie alwaies in two chambers over the said north church dour, for the same purpose that when any such offenders dyd come, and knocke, streight waie they were letten in, at any houre of the nyght, and dyd rynne streight waie to the Galleley Bell and tould it, to th' intent any man that hard it might knowe that there was som man that had taken Saunctuarie. And when the Prior had intelligence therof, then he dyd send word, and commanding them that they should keape themselves within the Saunctuarij, that is to saie within the Church and churchyard; and every one of them to have a gowne of blacke cloth maid with a cross of yeallowe cloth, called Sancte Cuthbert's cross, sett on his lefte shoulder of his arme, to th' intent that every one might se that there was such a frelige graunted by God and Sancte Cuthbert, for every such offender to flie unto for succour and safegard of there lyves, unto such tyme as they might obteyne their Prince's pardone, and that thei should lie within the Church or Saunctuarij in a GRATE, which grate ys remayninge and standing still to this daie, being maid onlie for the same purpose, standing and adjoining unto the Gallelei dore on the south syde, and likewise they had meite, drinke, and bedding, and other necessaries of the House cost and charg, for 37 daies, as was meite for such offenders, unto such tyme as the Prior and the Covent could gett theme conveyed out of the dioces.

CHAPTER IX

The Orders

IN the previous chapters the chief Orders of monks and regular canons have been referred to, but there has been no account of their constitution. An attempt must now be made to explain the main differences, coupled with a short sketch of monastic history.

The central principle of monasticism is retirement from the world. At specially corrupt times, when vice was unblushing, it has seemed to many good people to be a solemn duty to get away from the haunts of men, either alone or with others, to work out their own salvation and pray for the world. The monks have aimed at many other things—study, manual labour, hospitality, and so on—but the first and main principle of the whole system was retirement from the world.

There have been monks in most religions, such as the Essenes and Therapeutists among the Jews, and the Buddhist monks of Ceylon and Burma. In Christianity, the system took its rise in the third century, when Paul went into the desert of Egypt and founded the eremitic or hermit life. The most celebrated of the early monks was St Anthony, born in 251 of good family. At the age of 20 he sold his land and plunged into the desert, where for fifteen years he practised severe self discipline. He was followed by disciples who built their huts near his. The coenobitic system, or life in common, inevitably took the place of the anchoritic or life of complete withdrawal. St Anthony, without wishing it, became the first of the abbots, the head of a great community. He was a man of extraordinary influence, written to as a father by the Emperor Constantine and his sons. St Athanasius was his disciple and wrote his life. He died in 356 at the age of 105. Pacome, younger by forty years than Anthony but dead before him, had been a soldier under Constantine. He became a monk and practised great austerities, for fifteen years never lying down. He gave to the coenobites a written rule, the words of which he claimed to have been given to him by an angel. He founded at Tabenne in Upper Egypt the first proper monastery, or rather collection of eight monasteries, each governed by an abbot but united under a general superior. Before his death he ruled 3000 monks, and soon afterwards there were 7000 at his monasteries at Tabenne. St Jerome says that 50,000 were present at the annual gathering of those who followed his Rule. Near Arsinoë (Suez), Serapion governed 10,000. It has been asserted that there were in Egypt as many monks in the desert as there were inhabitants in the towns. At Oxyrhynchus on the Nile, in the year that St Anthony died, there were 10,000 monks and 20,000 virgins; so completely had the coenobitic system superseded the anchoritic.

Egyptian and oriental monasticism was very strict, with a terrible asceticism. Macarius the Alexandrine remained six months in the marshes constantly attacked by mosquitoes. Manual labour was much insisted on. When the elder Macarius visited St Anthony they set to work at mats while talking. Egyptian monasteries were called Laurae, from the Greek word meaning streets or lanes. At first there were rough irregular streets with single cells on either side. In time these became more regular and were enclosed by a wall. The plan of a Coptic monastery is descended from this arrangement.

St Basil flourished half a century after the death of St Anthony. His Rule takes the form of answers to 203 questions: it insists on absolute solitude, minute obedience, prohibition of personal property, and above all on labour as more important than fasting. Other great eastern monks were St Gregory of Nazianzus, "the father of Christian poetry," and St John Chrysostom, "the Christian Cicero," who wrote the best apology of the system, *Against the adversaries of Monastic Life*. After his time eastern monasticism greatly declined. In the west the system was introduced later but became still more flourishing. St Jerome and St Ambrose were supporters, and St Augustine too, greatly influenced by Athanasius' life of St Anthony. In 423 St Augustine wrote a Rule for nuns in twenty-four articles, which was revived later on under Charlemagne. The Rule of the regular canons was founded on his writings.

The Home of the Monk

After the middle of the fifth century, western monasticism declined sadly. There was no generally recognized Rule, and in many monasteries slackness was the least of the evils. The world outside was in a terrible condition; the whole of Italy had become a battlefield, and murder, rapine, and famine were rampant. Into such a world was born in the year 480 a man destined to have an influence quite incalculable, the great St Benedict. He came of a good family, who could afford to educate him well. At the age of 14 he went to the public schools of Rome, but the schools were filled with vice; license and crime were quite unchecked in the streets. The boy was shocked and fled. For a time he lived in an obscure village near Rome and then sought absolute solitude in the mountainous region of Sublacum, now Subiaco, some 40 miles away. Here he spent three years in a cave, from which reports of his saintly life were spread, many men flocking to learn from him. After a time he was elected abbot, against his will, of the neighbouring monastery of Vicovaro; but the monks were evil men and tried to poison him. He returned to Sublacum and built twelve small monasteries, giving to each a superior, while he governed all. Many miracles by his hands are recorded. Being again opposed by wicked men, he travelled further south, and about the year 529, on the confines of Campania, he founded on Monte Cassino a monastery destined to have a world-wide celebrity.

As a founder of monasteries, and even as a man of unusual sanctity, we might scarcely have heard of St Benedict. His main title to remembrance is his power as a lawgiver. The Rule he gave is immeasurably more important than any other in the west and has been called the *Magna Carta* of monasticism. It has often been referred to in the preceding chapters, covering as it does the whole monastic life. Its success is largely due to its consideration for human powers: the keynote is in the 48th chapter: "Let all things be done with moderation, however, on account of the fainthearted." St Pacome and St Basil legislated for the very austere, St Benedict for the average monk. It is true that some of the directions seem very severe to us, but they are mildness itself as compared with the oriental. Not that St Benedict put forward the Rule as the standard of perfection, but only as the minimum: it ends with the words:

Thou, therefore, whoever doth hasten to the celestial fatherland, perform with Christ's aid this Rule, written out as the least of beginnings: and then at length, under God's protection, thou wilt come to the greater things that we have mentioned; to the summits of learning and virtue.

Benedictine influence spread rapidly over western Europe, though quite two centuries went by before the Rule entirely superseded its rivals. In 1569 it was computed that there had been 37,000 Benedictine monasteries and that their inmates had included eleven emperors, twenty kings, fifteen sovereign dukes and electors, thirteen sovereign earls, nine empresses, and ten queens.

The Home of the Monk

In the Benedictine epoch and before, England was largely pagan, the home of missionary activity in the British Isles being Ireland, where before the close of the fifth century monasteries were thickly planted, which owed much to eastern models and the Rule of St Pacome. They consisted of a number of cells and small oratories built close together. Welsh monasteries were much the same: at Bangor Isycoed there were 3000 monks. The influence of Irish monks on their own countrymen was great, and on others, too, largely through St Columba, born in 521 and descended on both sides from Irish princely families. At the age of about 40 he founded the monastery of Iona in the Hebrides, a centre of light from which missionaries went forth, the chief being St Aidan, "the apostle of northern Britain." About the same time as these Celtic monks were active in the north, Benedictine monks arrived in the south, in 597, sent by Gregory the Great, himself a Benedictine who wished to be the Apostle of England. Augustine, the chief of the party, founded two monasteries at Canterbury, one of which, dedicated in honour of St Peter and St Paul, was afterwards called after him. In the seventh century the great light was St Cuthbert, Bishop of Lindisfarne, trained in Celtic ways but consecrated by Theodore, Archbishop of Canterbury. A little later Benedict Biscop, a nobly born and wealthy Northumbrian, founded the two monasteries of Jarrow and Wearmouth. The Venerable Bede, who died in 735, spent much of his life in both.

The seventh and eighth centuries saw the foundation of Tynemouth, Peterborough, Leominster, Wenlock, Whitby, Ely, Malmesbury, Evesham, and Sherborne. Glastonbury, as a British Christian settlement, is much older, but is said to have received the Benedictine Rule early in the seventh century. Speaking generally, however, the English monasteries at this time were only semi-monastic, and not really Benedictine. At the end of the eighth century and beginning of the ninth, Alcuin definitely received the Rule but was not able to secure its adoption in England. It was introduced or re-introduced at Glastonbury in the tenth century by Dunstan, a fervent Benedictine apologist. Canute founded many monasteries, the most important being Bury St Edmunds. The Benedictine triumph was not complete till after the Norman conquest. The semi-secular Saxon customs had to give way. For example, the canons of Durham were married. William de St Carileph, the second foreign bishop, substituted Benedictine monks, the canons being offered the alternative of leaving or putting away their wives. About 1077 Lanfranc promulgated his monastic Statutes, founded on the Use of the Abbey of Bec. About half of the mediaeval cathedrals were also Benedictine monasteries, an arrangement scarcely ever found out of England.

In early days it can hardly be said that there was a Benedictine "Order." St Benedict's idea was the reform of the whole monastic system and not the institution of one among rival Orders. Before long, however, a

83   6-2

weakness in the Benedictine polity became apparent, the entire separation of one abbey from another. All were at first subject to the bishops, but abbeys had no organic connexion with each other. The family life, with an abbot at the head, was a beautiful idea, but it fell to pieces if the abbot proved to be inefficient or immoral: episcopal control was often only nominal. Early in the ninth century an attempt was made to bring the units together, but there was no considerable reform till a hundred years later. In 910 the abbey of Cluni was founded by William, Duke of Aquitaine, with Berno as first abbot. The only thought at first was a return to the strict Rule of St Benedict, but soon the plan of dependent priories was instituted, all being subject to the Abbot of Cluni, who visited them and kept them up to the mark. The possible weakness of the Abbot of Cluni himself being a failure was ignored. The Cluniac Order spread widely over western Europe. There were 35 priories in England, Barnstaple being the earliest and Lewes the greatest. Other important houses were Wenlock, Northampton, Montacute, Castleacre. The Abbot of Cluni could not do all the supervision and delegated part of it to others. For example, Wenlock was immediately subject to La Charité sur Loire, which itself was subject to Cluni. There was a vicar general of the English province, usually the Prior of Lewes. The Order flourished greatly and succeeded, late in the eleventh century, in obtaining from the Pope exemption from episcopal control for all its houses. This *imperium in imperio* was of doubtful advantage to the Church at large. Whether influenced by it or not, Cluniac fervour sadly declined in the eleventh century. Like the Benedictines, the Cluniacs were called black monks, on account of their dress.

The next reform is of special interest as it was partly the work of an Englishman, Stephen Harding, a monk of Sherborne, born about 1070. On his way back from Rome, late in the century, he stayed at the abbey of Molesme in Burgundy. He found the monks living very slack lives, but Robert the abbot, Alberic the prior, and Stephen himself, tried to reform them, without avail. In 1098, with a few others, they left the abbey and took refuge in a wild wood under the protection of Odo, Duke of Burgundy. Here at Citeaux, or *Cistercium*, was founded the New Minster or *Novum Monasterium*, an abbey comparable in its importance with Monte Cassino. Molesme, though slack, wanted the lustre of Robert's presence, and he was sent back by the Pope a year later. Alberic became Abbot of Citeaux in 1099, and Stephen ten years later. They suffered frightful poverty, disease, and death. No novices joined and every one jeered. In 1112 or 1113 the tide turned. Thirty men, some middle-aged, and some young and noble, arrived at the gates of the monastery, led by a young man, twenty-three years of age. Of this leader at that period our accounts are not full. He was noble and well educated; he left the world and persuaded others also; he sought no gorgeous monastery but the poorest and strictest: there was success for Stephen at last. The leader was St Bernard, "the last of the Fathers," who is said to have had more influence on his age than any man who ever lived. Novices flocked to Citeaux, and colonization began. La Ferté was founded in 1113, Pontigny and Morimond in 1114, and Clairvaux, with St Bernard as abbot, in 1115. It is doubtful if the exiles of Molesme thought of a new Order, but after the crisis at Citeaux it became inevitable, under Stephen as abbot, and not Robert or Alberic. The constitution is contained in the *Carta Caritatis*, which shews a compromise between the Benedictine and Cluniac systems. The isolation of the former and the entire dependence of the latter are avoided. The Abbot of Citeaux was to visit the four daughter-houses, but was revisited in turn by their abbots. Each abbot visited the colonies of his own house, and the Abbot of Citeaux was *pater universalis ordinis*, and visited any abbey he liked. There was a General Chapter every year at Citeaux. As in the reform of 910 the underlying motive was a strict return to the Benedictine Rule, and, in this case, a protest against Cluniac pomp and luxury. At first there was no exemption from episcopal control, but the oath of allegiance was taken *salvo ordine nostro*, which gave room for different interpretations of the bishop's commands.

The Cistercian fervour soon spread to England, the first house being founded in 1129 at Waverley in Surrey. The minimum requirement was an abbot and

twelve monks, but these were secured over and over
again in the twelfth century, when Rievaulx, Fountains,
Roche, Kirkstall, Valle Crucis, Tintern, Buckfast, and
many another were founded. In the middle of the
twelfth century more than thirty monasteries of the
Order of Savigny, and including Furness, Byland,
Jervaulx, and Buildwas, joined the Cistercian or white
monks. So great was the popularity that the General
Chapter of 1152 forbade the foundation of any more
abbeys, though some were founded later.

Several Orders of Knighthood were loosely allied
to the Cistercians: the most important was the Knights
Templars, who were monks and knights combined.
Taking their rise at the time of the Crusades, their
original aim was to protect the pilgrims to Jerusalem,
and later permanently to guard the holy places. They
received a Rule from St Bernard.

The Cluniac discipline, and still more the Cistercian,
greatly affected the Benedictine. About 1132 many
abbots of the Province of Rheims agreed to meet
annually. In 1215 Innocent III, at the fourth Lateran
Council, attended by 412 bishops and nearly 1000
abbots, decreed the union of Benedictine monasteries.
In each province or kingdom all the abbots and regnal
priors were to meet every three years. While the
system was new, three Cistercian abbots were to be
invited, and they, with two of their own number, were
to preside. Thus the Benedictine General Chapter was
constituted.

The Home of the Monk

In 1086 the Carthusian Order had been founded by St Bruno of Cologne. There were only about ten houses in England, but the importance of the Order was great owing to its strictness and the long-continued faithfulness to its ideals. The most important priory in this country was the London Charterhouse, but the plan can now be most clearly studied at Mount Grace in Yorkshire. The buildings are hardly referred to in this book, which deals almost entirely with those of other Orders. The chief feature was a very large cloister, to which were connected small separate houses for the monks. The common dining hall was used only occasionally, and the church was much smaller than the normal. In almost complete silence the work was done. Flesh meat was not allowed, even to the sick and guests.

The Grandmontines had only three houses in England. They were founded about 1076 by St Stephen of Thiers and were almost confined to France: they became exempt from episcopal control in 1188. The churches were generally small and aisleless, with an apse at the east, broader than the rest of the building, even when apses as a rule had died out. The flesh of birds, as well as quadrupeds, was definitely forbidden.

So far, in this chapter, I have been speaking mainly of monks, but there were many other men in the Middle Ages living a cloistered life. About the middle of the eighth century, Chrodegang founded the regular canons. Most cathedral churches were served by secular canons, ordained priests who, like other secular clergy, mixed with the world and did not live by a special rule. The regular canons, however, lived in communities and were very like monks, except that all, or nearly all, were ordained, whereas monks might be laymen. In the early centuries, nearly all the monks were laymen, even St Benedict being only a deacon: in later times, most of them were ordained.

The most important of these semi-monastic Orders was the Augustinian, Austin, or black canons, not founded by St Augustine, but based on the 109th Epistle of his writings. They were probably introduced into England by Lanfranc.

The white canons had almost the same correspondence with the black canons as the white monks had with the black monks. They were founded about 1120 by St Norbert at Prémontré, near Laon. The Latin form of the name, *Premonstratensium*, was indicated by *pratum premonstratum*, the meadow supernaturally revealed to the founder. The Premonstratensians met in General Chapter, as the Austin canons did after a time. The former were exempt from episcopal jurisdiction.

Canons' houses in England were numbered by hundreds. One cathedral church, Carlisle, was served by Augustinians from the time of Henry I.

There was one purely English Order of regular canons, that of St Gilbert of Sempringham in Lincolnshire, founded in 1148. The special point was the association of men and women in the same priory, each with special cloister and buildings of their own, but joining in the church, though separated by stone screens. Watton in Yorkshire has been most fully excavated. St Gilbert founded thirteen houses, and there were twenty-six at the Dissolution.

There were women's branches of the other great Orders, notably the Benedictine and the Cistercian. The terms black nuns and white nuns were used, sometimes black ladies and white ladies. They are scarcely referred to in this book.

I have not found it possible to deal here with the friars, who are so often confused with the monks. They are really based on a different ideal, not retirement from the world, but service in the world. The most important Orders were the Franciscan, the Dominican, the Carmelite, the Augustinian. The first three are called grey, black and white friars, respectively. The buildings, at first non-existent or small and poor, gradually approximated to those of the monks, though retaining some characteristic differences.

The various Religious Orders had their vicissitudes, in fervour and prosperity, and their condition at one period is not a safe test of their condition at another. I cannot refrain from quoting the thirteenth century opinion as to some of them of Guyot de Provins, first a minstrel and afterwards a monk, who seems to have tried various Orders in turn. Of the Cluniacs he says:

When you wish to sleep they awake you; when you wish to eat, they make you fast. The night is passed in praying in the church, the day in working, and there is no repose but in the frater; and what is to be found there? Rotten eggs, beans with all their pods on, and liquor fit for oxen. For the wine is so poor, that one might drink of it for a month without intoxication.

Of the Carthusians:

I know the Carthusians, and their life does not tempt me. They have each their habitation; every one is his own cook; every one eats and sleeps alone; and I do not know whether God is much delighted with all this. But this I well know, that if I was myself in paradise, and alone there, I should not wish to remain in it. A solitary man is always subject to bad temper. Thus I call those fools, who wished me to immure myself in this way. But what I particularly dislike in the Carthusians is, that they are murderers of their sick. If these require any little extraordinary nourishment, it is peremptorily refused. I do not like religious persons who have no pity; the very quality which, I think, they especially ought to have.

Of the Cistercians:

The abbots and cellarers have ready money, eat large fish, drink good wine, and send to the frater, for those who do the work, the very worst. These monks I have seen put pig-sties in churchyards, and stables for asses in chapels. They seize the cottages of the poor, and reduce them to beggary.

Of the Grandmontines:

Besides fondness for good cheer, they were remarkable for the most ridiculous foppery. They painted their cheeks, washed and covered up their beards at night, as now women do their hair, in order that they might look handsome and glittering on the next day. They were entirely governed by the lay brethren, who got possession of their money; and with it, buying the Court of Rome, obtained the subversion of the Order.

Of the regular canons:

Augustine's Rule is more courteous than Benedict's. Among them, one is well shod, well clothed, well fed. They go out when they like, mix with the world, and talk at table.

The Home of the Monk

Of the Knights Hospitallers:

I have lived with them at Jerusalem, and have seen them proud and fierce. Besides, since by name and foundation they ought to be hospitable, why are they not so in reality? A monk in vain leads a very hard life, fasts, labours, chants, and reads the scriptures. If he is not charitable, it is only an uninhabited house, where the spider weaves his web.

Of the Knights Templars:

They are honoured in Syria, much dreaded by the Turks, and their Order would suit me well enough, were it not necessary to fight. But they are too brave. As for me, if I die, it will never be, I hope, through prowess or courage. I had rather be a living coward than have the most illustrious death in the whole world. These worthies of the Temple are very exact in all which concerns the service of the Church; and, respecting that point, I should yield to them in nothing; but the moment fighting commenced, they should go without me. A battle is not wholesome. I willingly leave that honour to them; and, please God, I hope to be neither killed nor wounded.

CHAPTER X

The Dissolution

WE have seen that the twelfth century was a time of earnestness and devotion, especially in the Cistercian Order. Late in the period, Abbot Aelred of Rievaulx says that he governed 300 monks, who drank water, ate little, worked hard, slept little and that on bare boards, never spoke except necessary words to a superior, and loved prayer. By the thirteenth century missionary zeal burned low, and the monks had become self-centred. The monasteries, however, were flourishing and still attracted large numbers, though earnest men, to a great extent, were joining the friars.

The fourteenth century was a period of decline, largely on account of the Black Death, which was most virulent in 1348–9 and lasted at least till 1357. Quite half the population of England are said to have been carried off, and the monks suffered in a peculiar degree. At Westminster the abbot and twenty-six monks died, and at Meaux 32 out of the 42 monks and all the *conversi*, seven in number. All this meant loss of wealth, lands untilled and unlet, worse still, the impossibility of keeping up the monastic services and fervour. There was an inevitable lack of continuity. The new importations, few in number, did not imbibe the old traditions.

The Home of the Monk

Another thing which weakened the monasteries was the disputes with secular clergy and laity. Many of the abbeys were good landlords and lived on friendly terms with their tenants, but there were plenty of exceptions. Two instances may be given. At Bury in 1327 there was a great riot of the townspeople and the secular clergy, who broke into the church and the cloister and even abused the sick monks in the infirmary. At Sherborne about 1435 there was a bitter dispute, mainly because the monks insisted on the lay folk bringing their children to the monastic church for baptism. In the riot which ensued, a secular priest shot a flaming arrow to some scaffolding, causing a great fire, the marks of which are evident to this day. The bickering of seculars and regulars was a constant scandal. Henry II visited a Cistercian abbey with Walter Map, Archdeacon of Oxford. In the chapter house the abbot said: "Sire, there is no place the devil hates so much as this. Here souls are reconciled, here our penances are performed, our offences punished." The reply of Map, a secular priest, was not complimentary: "No wonder that the devil hates the place where so many of his friends are whipped." One of the chief causes of the bitterness was the appropriation by the monks of parochial tithes, the favourite way of endowing monasteries by the king and nobles, with the connivance of the Pope and bishops. The usual thing was for the monastery to take some two-thirds, leaving only one-third for the vicar or substitute.

The Dissolution

Before the end of the fourteenth century, one third of the benefices in England were in the hands of monasteries, cathedrals, and colleges. In the contest Chaucer took the side of the parochial clergy. His monk and friar are far from desirable, but "the Poure Persone of a Town" is one of the most beautiful characters in literature.

After the twelfth century hardly any monasteries were founded. Popular enthusiasm was transferred to the friars in the thirteenth century, and in the fourteenth and fifteenth to colleges of secular clergy. These last were an attempt to combine the conventual and secular lives: priests lived together under a mild rule and were yet accessible to parochial needs and conducted dignified services in parish churches. There had been colleges long before, but the latter part of the Middle Ages was the great time for them. Monks very rarely, and regular canons infrequently, served parish churches, though the appointment of a vicar was often in the hands of a conventual foundation.

At the beginning of the sixteenth century it was quite natural that men should discuss whether the monasteries were serving a sufficient purpose or not. In the early days they had been missionary centres in the midst of pagan darkness, but that function had to a great extent passed away. At that time, and for long after, boys had been taught by the monks, either in the cloister itself or in schools specially founded.

Now many schools had been founded under the control of secular priests: even the monastic schools could be retained without the patron monasteries. The copying of ancient manuscripts, which filled so large a part of the monks' time in the early Middle Ages, was unnecessary after the invention of printing. The patronage of arts and crafts, and the work of landowning and farming, could obviously be entrusted to others. The *hospitium* could be exchanged for the inn, in the case of the well-to-do traveller. The monks, however, and they alone, made systematic provision for the poor. And what about the central feature of the monastic life, the worship of God? Could not that be observed without retirement from the world; nay, could men not pray better if they mixed with the world and found out its needs? Can anyone pray acceptably for so many hours a day as the monastic rule required? There is no doubt that the tedium was often found to be insupportable. Archbishop Winchelsey's Statutes of 1298 enforced attendance at extra masses on all who enjoyed the more generous fare in the *deportum*. Rather than attend the extra services many monks preferred not to eat in the *deportum*, and the Archbishop then made the masses compulsory and the *deportum* optional!

I am not claiming that all these arguments are of equal value, but the cumulative effect of them must have predisposed the men of the sixteenth century to consider the possibility of dissolution. The suppression of alien priories had long before been carried out,

though many had become denizen. As early as the time
of William I, English manors, with their churches and
tithes, had been given to Norman and French abbeys.
These built priories, which collected the revenues
and sent the bulk of them abroad. The number of
such priories grew to be more than one hundred, of
which the Cluniac were the most important. In the
time of Edward III these houses sent annually £2000
(quite £60,000 of our money) to Cluni. Before that,
King John had made the alien priories, then 81 in
number, pay him considerable sums of money. In 1294
Edward I seized them for his war expenses, and
Edward II followed suit. Edward III at first restored
some and then altered his mind. Finally, in 1414,
Henry V suppressed all which did not become denizen.
The king seems to have seized some; some were given
to other monasteries and to schools.

The exactions of kings were not confined to alien
priories; the monasteries as a whole were a convenient
stand-by when the sovereign was in difficulties. If the
king were giving his daughter in marriage, or wanted
money for any special object, the monasteries were
"invited" to contribute. Forced hospitality was
common enough. In 1199, according to Jocelyn,

King John immediately after his coronation, setting aside all
other affairs, came down to St Edmund, drawn thither by his
vow and by devotion. We, indeed, believed that he was come
to make offering of some great matter; but all he offered was
one silken cloth, which his servants had borrowed from our
sacrist, and to this day have not paid for. He availed himself

of the hospitality of St Edmund, which was attended with enormous expense, and upon his departure bestowed nothing at all either of honour or profit upon the saint, save thirteen easterling pence, which he offered at his mass on the day of his departure.

Henry VIII, therefore, had plenty of precedent, when he began to think of spoliation. In his youth he had a good opinion of the monasteries, but three reasons, apart from those given above, led him to take a different line. They opposed his divorce with Catharine of Aragon, they were the strongholds of papal obedience, and they were wealthy. It is true that they had never quite recovered from the Black Death, and that many had been mismanaged and got into debt, but the wealth was still enormous. Westminster, for example, had possessions in 97 towns and 17 villages, besides 216 manors. Cardinal Wolsey had obtained leave from the Pope to suppress several small monasteries to provide money for his two splendid colleges at Ipswich and Oxford. He followed, too, a vicious custom in holding St Albans *in commendam*, taking large revenues as titular abbot, and doing little or nothing for the abbey. Wolsey, however, might have acted as a check on the king if he had lived. His secretary and successor, Thomas Cromwell, was without scruples. He had seen how defenceless the monasteries were, and how easy it would be to raise large sums from them, and thus he began his wily and systematic attack. Commissions were sent round to examine the monasteries, and the results called *comperta* were sent in to Cromwell. These reports, in many cases but by no means all, picture a bad state of things, but how were they produced? The commissioners, Richard Layton, Thomas Legh, John London, John Ap Rice, were men of doubtful character. But, even if they had been trustworthy, their method would seriously reduce the value of the reports. The plan was to interview the inmates, try to get them to confess and then magnify the confession, persuade them to say they wished to leave the monastic life, holding out offers of preferment elsewhere, get them to incriminate each other, listen to malicious gossip from anyone, and then send in the reports. The truth of them was not tested, and the incriminated persons had no chance of reply. On such reports condemnation took place. If the commissioners could not find out anything, they said that the monks had evidently conspired together to tell nothing. What justice could be expected when men were paid to find abuses, and knew they would have to give way to others if they did not?

If therefore one had only the commissioners' reports to go by, we should have to suspend judgment on the state of the English monasteries. There is, however, other evidence. A committee of cardinals reported in 1538 as follows:

Another abuse which needs correction is in the religious orders, because they have deteriorated to such an extent that they are a grave scandal to seculars, and do the greatest harm by their example. We are of opinion that they should be all abolished, not so as to injure the vested interests of any one, but by forbidding them to receive novices; for in this wise they can be quickly done away with without wrong to anyone, and good religious can be put in their place. At present we think the best thing to be done is to dismiss all the unprofessed youths from their monasteries.

The best way to get at the truth is to study the bishops' visitations, of which we have many remaining. It is true that the Cistercian and Premonstratensian houses were exempt, but most of the Benedictine and Augustinian were subject to episcopal control. The exempt are not likely to have been better than the non-exempt. Take, for example, the diocese of Norwich, of which we have several visitation records between 1492 and 1532. On the whole, the monasteries were well conducted, but there were serious exceptions. At the Augustinian house of Walsingham in 1514 the prior was living a dissolute and scandalous life; he had robbed the treasury of money and jewels; he dressed as a layman; he kept a fool; he was immoral; he behaved towards the canons with violence and brutality. The canons themselves were dissipated and quarrelsome, and the pretence of religion was hardly kept up. The keeper of the shrine was absent from matins sixty times in the previous year; the servants were insolent and the boys mutinous. The canons frequented taverns and worse places; they hawked, hunted, and occasionally fought; they scaled walls and got out of bounds at forbidden hours. Some broke into the prior's cellar and stole his wine, and some sat up all night drinking, rolled into church in the early morning, and fell asleep and snored. The bishop naturally compelled the prior to resign. In 1526 things were better, but still no scholars were sent to the University, there was no pretence of educational work in the priory and no learning among the canons: the numbers had seriously fallen off. Walsingham was exceptionally bad, but here are faults of various monasteries, taken almost at random from the visitation of 1492:—no accounts given in, buildings out of repair, no schoolmaster, agriculture neglected, priory in debt (frequent), service books much worn, prior too easy, disorder and drunkenness, dissensions, frater not used, no seats in the cloister, no lights in the dorter, schoolboys neglected and allowed to keep sheep. On the other hand, it is often stated that no reform was needed, and that nothing required mending.

The bishops' visitations, though serious enough in many cases, do not reveal wholesale corruption, and if the king had depended entirely on them there would not have been sufficient cause for complete suppression. It was safer to rely on the commissioners, who could write in such a manner as this on their arrival in York: "This day we begin with St Mary's Abbey, whereat we suppose to find much evil disposition, both in the abbot and the convent, whereof, God willing, I shall certify you in my next letter."

Armed with the reports, the king went down to the parliament of 1536 and asked for the smaller monasteries to be suppressed. An Act was passed to do away with those whose income was under £200 a year. Many country gentlemen protested and bore witness to the value of the monasteries in their own neighbourhoods. There was more than one armed rising, the most important being the Pilgrimage of Grace in Yorkshire. Forty thousand men assembled under Robert Aske and other gentlemen. The revolt was soon stamped out by promise of pardon to the rank and file; the leaders were executed.

Having overcome all opposition, Henry VIII felt himself strong enough in 1538 to attack the greater abbeys, though the preamble of the Act of 1536 speaks of "divers and great solemn monasteries of this realm, wherein, thanks be to God, religion is right well kept and observed." The usual way of proceeding was to persuade the monks to resign, with promises of pension or preferment. It has been computed that in 1538 there were still 8081 religious in the country, but under 4000 were pensioned. The greater abbots received about £100 a year, and the ordinary monks £5 or £6. These sums must be multiplied by about 20 to represent our own money. If the abbots would not resign and would not accept the king's ecclesiastical supremacy, there was short shrift for them. The three most celebrated were Abbot Whiting of Glastonbury, Abbot Cook of Reading, and Abbot Marshall or Becke of Colchester. These could not be induced to submit by threats or bribery and so suffered death. The judges, like the Parliament, carried out the king's will all too readily, and within two years the suppression was complete. Among the monks the Carthusians had been the special opponents of the royal supremacy of the Church, and were therefore treated with special cruelty.

The revenues of the monasteries have been computed as about £150,000 a year, say three millions of our money. In addition, large sums were realized by the sale of ornaments, vestments, lead, bells, furniture, etc. The money was not all spent selfishly; much went to guns, ships, and coast fortifications, but much also on the king's personal expenditure, on the Prince of Wales's household, and on the royal palaces. The king had promised Parliament that many new bishoprics should be founded and that old cathedral priories should be turned into new cathedral colleges. The latter promise was fulfilled as regards the Augustinian priory of Carlisle and the Benedictine priories of Canterbury, Durham, Ely, Norwich, Rochester, Winchester, and Worcester. The cathedral abbey of Bath became a parish church, but the cathedral priory of Coventry was destroyed. The king planned more than a dozen new sees and cathedrals, but only five were carried out: Chester, Gloucester, Peterborough, which had been Benedictine abbeys; Bristol, and Osney (afterwards Christ Church, Oxford), formerly Augustinian. In addition, Westminster, where the king's parents were buried, became cathedral, though the bishopric lasted only ten years.

In a few cases, monastic churches were not destroyed and became parochial, even though the parishioners had to buy them: St Albans, Sherborne, and Tewkesbury are good examples. In a great many others, the nave of the monastic church had parochial rights and was left alone, even when the eastern part was pulled down: Shrewsbury, Waltham, Dunstable, Lanercost, Bolton are instances. At Hexham, the quire and transept were preserved. However, in the large majority of cases the ruin was almost complete, even including such splendid and historic examples as Bury St Edmunds, Evesham, and St Mary's at York. The Premonstratensian and Cistercian churches were specially unfortunate, being far removed from the haunts of men. Cistercian naves, however, are now used as parish churches at Holme Cultram and Margam, a Cistercian presbytery at Dore, a Cistercian frater at Beaulieu, and the *capella extra portas* at four or five other places. Very many were fitted up as gentlemen's mansions, such as the Austin canonesses' house at Lacock. The church, in such cases, was usually pulled down, but there is one striking exception, at Bromfield in Shropshire. Here the nave was parochial and the presbytery Benedictine. The grantee at the Dissolution incorporated the presbytery into his private house and his grandson restored it: two domestic windows may still be seen in the east wall.

Even in ruin, however, the charm of the monasteries can hardly be resisted. There are few more beautiful

PLATE XX

RIEVAULX

sights than Tintern, Furness, Fountains, Rievaulx. An American is said to have observed to an Englishman: "What thoughtful people your ancestors were; they not only built churches for you to worship in but ruined abbeys for you to admire." No, they were not always ruins! There was a time when the abbeys of England stood proudly with no thought of the coming storm; when the monks and canons day by day were worshipping God according to their lights, were teaching the children as their knowledge allowed, were foremost in the arts and sciences, were ruling large territories with kindness and wisdom, were feeding the hungry, and clothing the naked, and welcoming the stranger. And if there is a dark side to the picture, if corruption crept in, if the Rule of St Benedict began to be thought old and somewhat strait, if the evil world could not be excluded altogether from the cloister, let our judgment be as merciful as truth will allow, let us remember that the monks were men of like passions as ourselves. Given the same conditions, the same opportunities, the same temptations, should we be any better than they?

Even if we believe the whole theory of monasticism a false one, even if we think the monks fell far short of their own ideal, even if we credit all the charges against them, it would still be ungrateful for any Englishman, yes for any Christian, to forget the debt he owes to the monks of the Middle Ages.

Plans

This plan is founded on that drawn by the late Sir William St John Hope and is printed by permission of Lady Hope. The original, from which many details have been omitted, is reproduced in the Surtees Society's edition of 1903 of *The Rites of Durham*.

The cathedral and abbey church is mainly of Norman date. The Galilee, at the west end, was added late in the twelfth century, and the Chapel of the Nine Altars, at the east end, about the middle of the following century.

Much of the east and south ranges of the claustral buildings dates from early Norman times: the eastern part of the chapter house, destroyed in 1796, has recently been rebuilt on the old plan. The west range was rebuilt in the thirteenth century; the cloister itself in the fifteenth, the tracery dating from the eighteenth. The prior's lodging, now the Deanery, contains work of various periods. The great kitchen dates from the latter part of the reign of Edward III.

The extra-claustral buildings are not complete, though surviving to a greater extent than in most other abbeys. The gateway was rebuilt not long before the Dissolution.

Plans

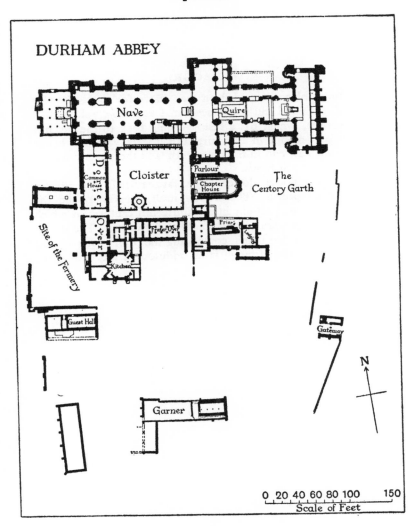

DURHAM ABBEY

Nave

Quire

Cloister

Parlour

Common House

Chapter House

The Centory Garth

Dorter Over

Site of the Fermery

Frater Use

Prior's Lodging

Kitchen

Guest Hall

Gateway

N

Garner

0 20 40 60 80 100   150
Scale of Feet

107

Plans

WENLOCK

This Cluniac plan is founded on that drawn for the author by Mr P. W. Hubbard and reproduced in *Archaeologia*, vol. LXXII.

The church, which has a history going back to the seventh century, was rebuilt in the thirteenth, the lady chapel being added at the east end in the fourteenth, and the sacristy on the south side in the fifteenth.

The chapter house, dorter range, farmery hall, and cloister lavatory are Norman. The cloister itself, the frater, and the western range were rebuilt in the thirteenth century, in which further buildings were erected south of the dorter. The south-eastern range, in two floors, comprising the prior's lodging and an extension of the farmery, is an addition of the end of the fifteenth century.

Plans

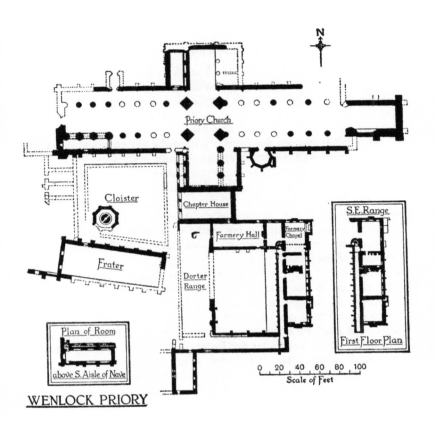

N

Priory Church

Cloister

Chapter House

Farmery Hall

Farmery Chapel

S.E. Range

Frater

Dorter Range

First Floor Plan

Plan of Room above S. Aisle of Nave

WENLOCK PRIORY

0 20 40 60 80 100
Scale of Feet

Plans

KIRKSTALL

The plan is founded on that used in the *Thoresby Society Publications*, vol. XVI, for the late Sir William St John Hope's article on Kirkstall Abbey, with the supplementary essay by Mr John Bilson on the Architecture of the Cistercians. It is here printed by permission of Lady Hope and Mr Bilson.

Kirkstall is chosen for illustration, as the Cistercian arrangements of the twelfth century are more completely shewn in that abbey than elsewhere. The presbytery has not had aisles added, as in so many other cases, and the transeptal chapels are unaltered. The position of the frater, running north and south, with warming house on the east and kitchen on the west, is the normal Cistercian one. The lay brethren, as usual, occupied most of the western range. East of it was the "lane," the use of which is discussed on p. 32.

The plan of the eastern range is wonderfully complete, but the chapter house was extended eastwards in the thirteenth century. Alterations to the infirmary took place in the fifteenth century, in which period a meat kitchen was added at the southeast corner of the frater range: the misericorde, or hall for the eating of meat, was under the frater. The abbot's lodging was, as usual in the Cistercian Order, adjoining the dorter range. The buildings on the south side of the infirmary were probably the lodging of the visiting abbot from Citeaux or one of the four daughter houses.

Plans

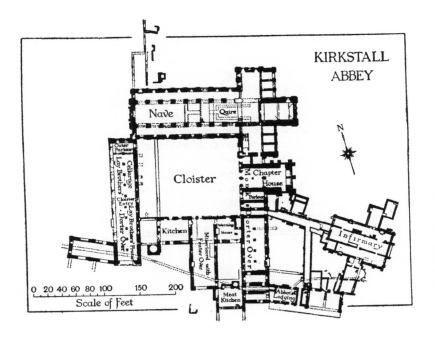

III

Plans

HAVERFORDWEST

The plan is founded on those by Mr A. W. Clapham and Mr Ernest A. R. Rahbula in *Archaeologia Cambrensis* (December 1921 and December 1924). It is printed here by permission of Mr Clapham and the Cambrian Archaeological Association.

Houses of regular canons, whether Augustinian as in this case or Premonstratensian, are often smaller and less important than those of the Benedictine, Cluniac, and Cistercian Orders. Some of the churches are aisleless and some have only one aisle.

The buildings date mainly from the thirteenth century, with some additions of later periods. The claustral ranges are of normal character. The kitchen is rather farther from the frater than usual. The position of the farmery was always a matter of local convenience, the quietest part of the monastery being chosen.

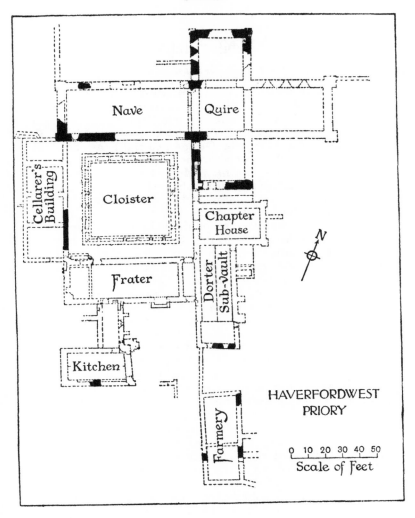

HAVERFORDWEST
PRIORY

Scale of Feet

Bibliography

(The bibliography is not indexed)

THE most important document with regard to western monastic life is the Rule of St Benedict, which has often been printed. Most of it, translated into English, will be found in *Select Historical Documents of the Middle Ages,* edited by E. F. Henderson and published by George Bell and Sons. Some of the other Rules will be found in one of the greatest books ever published, Dugdale's *Monasticon Anglicanum,* 1655–1673. The best edition (8 vols. folio) is that published in 1817–1830, which has, in addition to the Latin original, a history of each religious foundation in English: it is of course out of print. The most important rules, etc., for one of the chief Orders have been printed in *Cistercian Statutes* by the late Rev. Canon J. T. Fowler: they are not translated, but there are some valuable notes in English. This was reprinted from the *Yorkshire Archaeological Journal* in 1890, and a second-hand copy can occasionally be obtained. The Rule of St Augustine, for regular canons, is contained in *The Observances in use at the Augustinian Priory of S. Giles and S. Andrew at Barnwell, Cambridgeshire,* by J. Willis Clark. Unfortunately, only a small edition of this valuable book was printed, and it is difficult to obtain. The Customs of the Priory are also printed in it in both Latin and English, and throw great light on mediaeval monastic life. Other Rules and Books of Customs have been published in Latin only. An English abstract of the Consuetudinary of the Benedictine Abbey of St Augustine at Canterbury is printed in the Rev. E. L. Taunton's *The English Black Monks of St Benedict,* published by J. C. Nimmo. A contemporary account of life in a large monastery at the end of the twelfth century is given in the *Chronicles of Jocelyn of Brakelond.* The original Latin was published by the Camden Society in 1840, and there are several English translations. A convenient one is published by Chatto and Windus. The *Chronicles* have been popularized by Carlyle in *Past and Present,* Book II. Of a different type, but also illustrating monastic polity, are the business records of a monastery, often printed in the *Monasticon*, or published separately as in the case of *Sacrists' Rolls of Ely*, edited by F. R. Chapman, and privately printed.

Much information on monastic life is given in the Bishops' Visitations. Some of these have been published in Latin, but for the Diocese of Lincoln, 1420 to 1449, an excellent English translation has been made by Professor Hamilton Thompson in the Visitations he has edited for the Lincoln Record Society. See also *Visitations of English Cluniac Foundations*, by Sir G. F. Duckett, Bart., and *Visitations of the Diocese of Norwich*, 1492 to 1532, edited by Dr Jessopp for the Camden Society in 1888. *Letters relating to the Suppression of the Monasteries*, edited by Thomas Wright, was published by the Camden Society in 1843.

The most important original authority in reference to monastic buildings is a book written in 1593, which goes by the name of *The Rites of Durham*. It contains a very careful and interesting description, in English, of the monastery of Durham before its dissolution in 1539. The book was published by the Surtees Society in 1845, and again in 1903. Both editions can sometimes be obtained second-hand. The later has many valuable notes by the late Canon Fowler, and two fine coloured plans by the late Sir William St John Hope.

The accurate study of monastic buildings was really founded by Professor Willis, who wrote several monographs on the subject, notably *The Architectural History of the Conventual Buildings of Christ Church in Canterbury*, published by the Kent Archaeological Society in 1869, and now scarce and out of print. It contains a tracing of a Norman drawing of the monastery made about the year 1165. The late Sir William Hope wrote a wonderful series of monographs on monastic buildings, of which the following are specially important: *The Architectural History of the Cathedral Church and Monastery of St Andrew at Rochester*, published by Mitchell and Hughes in 1900; "Fountains Abbey" in the *Yorkshire Archaeological Journal*, vol. xv.; "The Abbey of St Mary-in-Furness" in the *Transactions* of the Cumberland and Westmorland Antiquarian and Archaeological Society, vol. XVI.

Monographs on the same subject by living authors have been numerous. Many of these are in *The Victoria History of the Counties of England*. *Archaeologia*, the quarto publication of the

The Home of the Monk

Society of Antiquaries, contains the following: *Lacock Abbey, Wilts*, by Harold Brakspear (vol. LVII); *The Cistercian Abbey of Stanley, Wiltshire*, by Harold Brakspear (vol. LX); *The Plan of the Church and Monastery of St Augustine, Bristol*, by Roland W. Paul (vol. LXIII); *Malmesbury Abbey*, by Harold Brakspear (vol. LXIV); *The Monastery of St Milburge at Much Wenlock, Shropshire*, by D. H. S. Cranage (vol. LXXII); *The Architecture of the Premonstratensians, with special reference to their Buildings in England*, by A. W. Clapham (vol. LXXIII); *The Order of Grandmont and its Houses in England*, by Rose Graham and A. W. Clapham (vol. LXXV).

The Archaeological Journal, published by the Royal Archaeological Institute, contains the following: *The Benedictine Nunnery of Little Marlow*, by C. R. Peers (vol. LIX); *Burnham Abbey, Bucks*, by Harold Brakspear (vol. LX); *The Architecture of the Cistercians with special reference to some of their earlier Churches in England*, by John Bilson (vol. LXVI); *Wigmore Abbey*, by Sir William Hope and Sir Harold Brakspear (vol. XC). The *Journal* of the British Archaeological Association contains the following: *The Premonstratensian Abbey of Langley, Co. Norfolk*, by F. C. Elliston Erwood (vol. XXVIII, new series). There are a number of shorter accounts in the same journal. Many other articles on religious houses are contained in the *Transactions* of local archaeological societies; some of the more important are mentioned in the course of this article.

Westminster Abbey has been dealt with from various points of view, architectural and monastic, in recent years. See "Further Notes on the Abbey Buildings at Westminster," by J. T. Micklethwaite in vol. LI of *The Archaeological Journal*; *Westminster Abbey*, by Francis Bond, published by Henry Frowde; *William de Colchester, Abbot of Westminster*; *The Monks of Westminster*; *Walter de Wenlock, Abbot of Westminster*, by E. H. Pearce, Bishop of Worcester, the first and third published by the S.P.C.K., the second by the Cambridge University Press; *Westminster Abbey and the King's Craftsmen* and *Westminster Abbey re-examined*, by W. R. Lethaby, both published by Duckworth and Co.; *Westminster Abbey*, as vol. I of *An Inventory of the Historical Monuments in London*, published by the Royal Commission; *Westminster Abbey: the Church, Convent, Cathedral, and College of St Peter, Westminster*, by H. F. Westlake, published by Philip Allan and Co.

Bibliography

Another great house has recently been thoroughly treated by T. D. Atkinson, *An architectural history of the Benedictine Monastery of Saint Etheldreda at Ely*, sumptuously produced by the Cambridge University Press.

Several general books on monastic life and buildings have been written. Cardinal Gasquet's *English Monastic Life* (Methuen and Co.) contains a list of English religious houses, with marks to shew where remains still exist. A much fuller list, with considerable notes of remains, is in *Church Work and Life in English Minsters* by Mackenzie E. C. Walcott, published by Chatto and Windus, and long out of print. *English Monasteries*, by Professor Hamilton Thompson, published by the Cambridge University Press, contains a succinct account of the Orders and of the chief buildings of a monastery. Another book, of great charm, is *Abbeys* (on the Great Western Railway), by Dr M. R. James, Provost of Eton, with a chapter on monastic life by Professor Hamilton Thompson. For the Gilbertine Order, see Miss Rose Graham's *St Gilbert of Sempringham and the Gilbertines*, published by Elliot Stock. The same author has written also on the Cluniacs: see especially "The English Province of the Order of Cluny in the fifteenth century," in vol. VII of the *Transactions* of the Royal Historical Society. For the white monks, see "The Cistercian Order," by J. T. Micklethwaite, in *The Yorkshire Archaeological Journal*, vol. XV.

For monastic history, several articles in the *Encyclopaedia Britannica* should be consulted, and the *Cambridge Medieval History*, vol. I, pp. 521–542, by Dom E. C. Butler, Abbot of Downside. Count Montalembert's great work, *The Monks of the West*, is delightful reading though not altogether trustworthy. It stops with the twelfth century, though the introduction and that of Cardinal Gasquet in the English edition give a brief sketch of monastic history in mediaeval and modern days. An excellent general sketch, published by George Allen and Unwin, is Mr Ian C. Hannah's *Christian Monasticism*. For the Dissolution period, see Cardinal Gasquet's *Henry VIII and the English Monasteries* (J. C. Nimmo), and the criticism of Mr G. G. Coulton, *The Monastic Legend*, published by Simpkin, Marshall, Hamilton, Kent and Co. In several of his larger books Mr Coulton has also dealt with monastic history: see, for example, *Five Centuries of Religion*.

The Home of the Monk

British Monachism, by T. D. Fosbrooke (new edition, published in 1817), will always be valuable on account of its frequent reference to original authorities. It gives, in an English translation, the opinions of the various Orders by Guyot de Provins in the thirteenth century.

Index

Index

Monte Cassino, 9, 80, 85
More, Sir Thomas, 17
Morimond, 39, 86
Mount Grace, 88
Music, 51

necessarium, the, 20
Newminster, 28, 67
"Nine men's morris," 2
Norwich, 2, 4, 5, 13, 29, 40, 63, 103
Novices, 2 f., 10, 28
Nunneries, 90

O Sapientia, feast of, 27
Obits, 14
Orders, the monastic, 77–92
Organ(s), the 72
Oxford, Gloucester Hall, 9; St Bernard's College, 10; St Frideswide, Priory of, 10; St John's College, 10; Trinity College, 9; Worcester College, 9
Oxyrhynchus, 78

Painted glass, 67
Paris, Matthew, 9, 18, 40
Parish churches, 104
Parlour, the, 12, 35
Paul the hermit, 77
Peterborough, 46, 71, 83, 103
Pilgrimage of Grace, 102
Pilgrims, 57, 58, 70, 87
pistrinum, 60
Pittances, 27 f., 49
pittensarius, 28
plumbarium, 60
Pontigny, 39, 86
Porter, the, 2, 56
Precentor, the, 6
Premonstratensian canons, 89
Prior, the, 40, 45
Prison, the, 16, 57
Property, Benedictine Rule and, 12 f.
Pulpits, 24
pulpitum, 72 f.
Punishments, 15

Reading on Sunday, 6 f.; at meals, 24 f.
refectorium, 22 ff., *see* Frater
Relics, 70
Reredorter, 20, 32
Richard de Sudbury, 42
Rievaulx, 13, 57, 62, 65, 68, 73, 74, 87, 93, 105
Robert de Insula, 40
Rochester, 40, 103

Sacrist, sacristy, 70 f.
St Albans, 7, 9, 18, 23, 40, 41, 71, 75, 98, 104
St Bernard's College, Oxford, 10
St Frideswide, Oxford, Priory of, 10
St Gall, 13, 22, 30, 59
St Jerome quoted, 78, 79
St John's College, Oxford, 10
Saints:
Aidan, 82; Ambrose, 79; Anthony, 77, 79; Athanasius, 78, 79; Augustine, 79, 82; Basil, 79, 81; Benedict, 9, 89 (Rule quoted, 3–42 *passim*, 56, 59, 64, 80, 81, 105); Bernard, 32, 86; Bruno, 88; Columba, 7, 82; Cuthbert, 7, 69, 82; Dunstan, 7, 83; Edmund, 28, 69, 70; Edward (the Confessor), 69; Ethelwold, 26; Gilbert of Sempringham, 89; Gregory of Nazianzus, 79; John Chrysostom, 79; Lawrence, 70; Macarius, 79; Martin, 54; Norbert, 89; Pacome, 78, 81, 82; Peter, 70; Stephen of Thiers, 88; Thomas (Becket), 69, 70; Wolstan, 69
Salerno, University of, 9
Salisbury, 13
Sampson, Abbot of Bury, 11, 13, 42, 43, 52, 53, 58
Sanctuary, right of, 76
"Screens," 30
scriptorium, 3 ff., 6
sempectae, the, 47
Serapion, 78
Sermons, 14
Shap, 74

Index

CAMBRIDGE: PRINTED BY W. LEWIS, M.A., AT THE UNIVERSITY PRESS

For EU product safety concerns, contact us at Calle de José Abascal, 56–1°, 28003 Madrid, Spain or eugpsr@cambridge.org.

www.ingramcontent.com/pod-product-compliance
Ingram Content Group UK Ltd.
Pitfield, Milton Keynes, MK11 3LW, UK
UKHW012342130625
459647UK00009B/471